TALKABOUT

Second Edition

A SOCIAL COMMUNICATION SKILLS PACKAGE

ALEX KELLY

www.speechmark.net

First published in 2016 by
Speechmark Publishing Ltd, 2nd Floor, 5 Thomas More Square, London E1W 1YW, UK
Tel: +44 (0)845 034 4610 Fax: +44 (0)845 034 4649
www.speechmark.net

© Alex Kelly, 2016

All rights reserved. The whole of this work, including all text and illustrations, is protected by copyright. No part of it may be copied, altered, adapted or otherwise exploited in any way without express prior permission, unless in accordance with the provisions of the Copyright Designs and Patents Act 1988 or in order to photocopy or make duplicating masters of those pages so indicated, without alteration and including copyright notices, for the express purpose of instruction and examination. No parts of this work may otherwise be loaded, stored, manipulated, reproduced, or transmitted in any form or by any means, electronic or mechanical, including photocopying and recording, or by any information storage and retrieval system, without prior written permission from the publisher, on behalf of the copyright owner.

Designed and typeset by Moo Creative (Luton)
002-6062/Printed in the United Kingdom by Hobbs the printers
British Library Cataloguing in Publication Data
A catalogue record for this book is available from the British Library

ISBN 978 1 91118 624 3

TALKABOUT

Contents — Page

Acknowledgements		5
About the author		5
Preface to the second edition		6
Introduction	This section includes a brief introduction to the book and the theory behind Talkabout. It also includes some practical suggestions for intervention, including setting up and running a group.	7
Assessment	This section includes an assessment of self-awareness and self-esteem, an assessment of social skills and a planning sheet for intervention.	19
Level 1 Talkabout Body Language	The aim of the topics in this section is to improve body language. This includes activities to develop skills in: eye contact, facial expression, gesture, distance, touch, fidgeting, posture and personal appearance.	33
Level 2 Talkabout The Way We Talk	The aim of this topic is to improve the way we talk (paralinguistic skills). This includes activities to develop skills in: volume, rate, clarity, intonation and fluency.	133
Level 3 Talkabout Conversations	The aim of the topics in this section is to improve conversational skills. This includes activities to develop skills in: listening, starting a conversation, taking turns, asking questions, answering questions, being relevant, repairing, and ending a conversation.	167
Level 4 Talkabout Assertiveness	The aim of the topics in this section is to improve assertiveness skills. This includes activities to develop skills in: expressing feelings, standing up for yourself, making suggestions, refusing, disagreeing, complaining, apologising, and requesting explanations.	235

Group cohesion games	This section contains a few suggestions for group cohesion games to play at the start or the end of sessions.	**321**
Record forms	This section contains various forms which can be used for session planning and evaluation.	**323**
References		**328**
Index	This lists the topics and the associated activities.	**329**

Acknowledgements

In the past 30 years I have had the pleasure of working in a job and speciality that I love and so many people have helped me along the way. I am grateful to the NHS and all my NHS colleagues for the 23 years of experience of working for such an amazing organisation. I certainly would not be the person or therapist I am today without those years. Now I am grateful to the people who believe enough in me, to come and work for me ... and there are now 19 of us.

So thank you to my lovely staff team – particularly to Naomi Pearson and Rebecca Elwell, who manage the teams so well, and to Amy Green, who helps me with all the social skills work. Amy – yet again, I have to thank you for your support in writing a book! I wouldn't want to have written it without you. And thank you to the rest of the team: to Grace Anstey, Jo Bartholomew, Amy Bigwood, Joley Blunden, Sophie Chamberlain, Lisa Davidson, Marnie Daws, Emily Dennis, Nevin Gouda, Amy Keable, Chris McLoughlin, Zara Owens, Helen Smith and Hayley Tutton. I believe we are truly making a difference in everything we do and I want to thank you all for your enthusiasm, dedication and hard work.

This book is dedicated to the men in my life. To my children Ed, Pete and George – I am so proud of you all. And to my husband (and business partner) Brian Sains – I love you.

Alex Kelly
(October 2015)

About the author

Alex Kelly is a Speech and Language Therapist with 30 years of experience working with both children and adults with an intellectual disability (learning disability), and specialising in working with people who have difficulties with social skills. She runs her own business (Alex Kelly Ltd) with her husband Brian Sains and is the author of several books and resources, including the best-selling TALKABOUT series.

Alex Kelly Ltd, based in Hampshire, England, provides training and consultancy work to schools and organisations in social skills around the UK and abroad. The company also provides speech and language therapy in schools in and around Hampshire. Finally, there is a day service for adults called 'Speaking Space' which aims to support people with social and communication skills difficulties through group work.

You can contact Alex through her website: **www.alexkelly.biz**

Preface to the second edition

TALKABOUT was first published 20 years ago in 1996 and this second edition has been on my list of things to do for about five years. My interest and passion in working with people with social skills difficulties started as soon as I qualified in the mid-1980s and the first edition of Talkabout was written following a clinical study of social skills, which I completed between 1991 and 1995. It was the first social skills package to give people a hierarchy to work through and included basic worksheets for all areas and skills that you would cover when working with someone.

Since then, my work in this field has developed and increased and, along with this, so have the Talkabout products. Each Talkabout book is now aimed at a specific client group – for example, with secondary mainstream pupils, you can use the *Talkabout for Teenagers* book and for primary children, the Talkabout for Children series. Each book has become more activity-based with suggestions for games and activities for each topic. They are also more of a complete intervention package for teachers and therapists to use, including a scheme of work for teachers to follow throughout an academic year.

The other development came in 2004 when I changed the hierarchy to include self-esteem and friendship skills. So the newer Talkabout books address not only self-awareness and social skills but also self-esteem and friendship skills.

So the time has come to update the original book to include more activities, more drawings and more suggestions, which are now based on my 30 years of experience of working in this area. I have also linked it with the other resources that are available so that you can use it as successfully as possible.

I hope you like the new book but, more importantly, I hope you find it useful.

Alex Kelly
August 2015

Please feel free to contact me for more information or help with your social skills work. My website is **www.alexkelly.biz**

TALKABOUT Introduction

Introduction

Overview

Talkabout is a practical resource that has been designed to help therapists and teaching staff to teach social skills in a more structured way, giving ideas on the process of intervention with lots of activities and worksheets to use at every stage. It is aimed at working with people in groups but it can also be adapted for working on a one-to-one basis.

The book is divided into the following sections.

Assessment

This section includes two assessments: a quick assessment of someone's self-awareness and a social skills assessment. From here you can decide where to start your intervention. If you decide that the person needs self-awareness and self-esteem work, you will need to use the book *Talkabout for Adults: developing self awareness and self esteem*. If the person needs social skills work, you can choose which of the four levels of this book to start at.

Level 1 Body Language

This level aims to improve body language and includes activities and worksheets on eight topics: eye contact, facial expression, gesture, distance, touch, posture, fidgeting and personal appearance.

Level 2 The Way We Talk

This level aims to improve paralinguistic skills and includes activities and worksheets on five topics: volume, rate, clarity, intonation and fluency.

Level 3 Conversations

This level aims to improve conversational skills and includes activities and worksheets on eight topics: listening, starting a conversation, taking turns, asking questions, answering questions, relevance, repairing and ending a conversation.

Level 4 Assertiveness

This level aims to improve assertiveness skills and includes activities and worksheets on eight topics: expressing feelings, standing up for yourself, making suggestions, refusing, disagreeing, complaining, apologising and requesting explanations.

TALKABOUT Introduction

Forms and group cohesion ideas

At the end of the book there are several ideas and forms to help with planning and evaluating your work, including some new group cohesion games and activities.

Who Talkabout is aimed at

Talkabout was originally developed and designed to be used with children and adults with social skills difficulties and this has not changed. It has now been adapted to be fairly generic in its usability but is most ideal for use in secondary special schools or ASD (autism spectrum disorder) units or with adults.

The table below summarises the Talkabout books and which ones to use with different ages and client groups.

Summary of the Talkabout resources

Resource	What it includes	Age range	Particularly suited to …
Talkabout Assessment CD (2010)	An assessment wheel on a CD Rom	All	Anyone
Talkabout 2nd edition (2016)	An assessment of social skills Activities and worksheets for four areas of social skills: Body Language, The Way We Talk, Conversations, Assertiveness	All	Secondary-aged pupils in special schools or units Adults with intellectual disability or ASD
Talkabout for Adults: developing self-awareness and self-esteem (2014)	An assessment of self-awareness and self-esteem A year's worth of activities and worksheets to develop self-awareness and self-esteem	16 years upwards	Adults with intellectual disability or ASD Older secondary pupils in special schools or units
Talkabout for Teenagers (2009)	A screening tool for self-esteem, social skills and friendship skills Five modules on self-esteem, social skills and friendship skills	10–25 years	Secondary-aged pupils in mainstream schools Young adults with high functioning ASD

Resource	What it includes	Age range	Particularly suited to ...
Talkabout for Children 1: developing self-awareness and self-esteem (2011a)	An assessment of self-awareness and self-esteem. One year's worth of activities and worksheets to develop self-awareness and self-esteem	4–16 years	Primary-aged pupils in mainstream schools. Children with an intellectual disability (all ages)
Talkabout for Children 2: developing social skills (2011b)	An assessment of social skills. Two years' worth of activities and worksheets to develop body language, conversations and assertiveness	4–16 years	Primary-aged pupils in mainstream schools. Children with an intellectual disability (all ages)
Talkabout for Children 3: friendship skills (2013)	One year's worth of activities and worksheets to develop friendship skills	4–16 years	Primary-aged pupils in mainstream schools. Children with an intellectual disability (all ages)
Talkabout Cards (2011d)	Two sets of cards for group cohesion activities and self-awareness games	All	Anyone
Talkabout DVD (2006)	Video clips of inappropriate and appropriate social skills. Includes all of the skills worked on in Talkabout	7 years upwards	Anyone except very young children
Talkabout Posters (2011c)	A set of 16 posters illustrating the key steps to success for social skills	All	Anyone
Talkabout Board Game (2011)	A board game for children to play at different levels, including self-esteem, body language, assertiveness, etc	7 years upwards	Anyone
Talkabout Relationships (2004)	An assessment of self-esteem and relationship skills. Sections on developing self-esteem and developing relationships	18 years upwards	Older children and adults with a mild to moderate intellectual disability

The theory behind Talkabout

Talkabout was first developed in the early 1990s when I was working as a speech and language therapist in London, UK. I was particularly interested in social skills but was frustrated by two aspects of my work as a therapist. First, there was nothing in the literature to guide me on where to start intervention following assessment; and second, my experience showed me that I was not always successful in what I was trying to teach and I could not always predict which children were going to improve and which were not. I set about to solve these two problems over a period of four years.

I started my investigations at a college of further education where I was working with 60 students who had a mild to moderate intellectual disability. We assessed all of the young people I was working with using an adapted social skills assessment from the Personal Communication Plan by Alex Hitchings and Robert Spence – now published in Kelly (2000). The students were involved in this assessment which gave us some insight into their own awareness of their difficulties. From these initial results, we grouped students into their main area of need: body language, conversational skills and assertiveness. We evaluated success through retesting on the original assessment and also compared students with poor and good awareness of their needs.

The results were fascinating. They showed that the students who had been working on their conversational skills progressed more if they had good existing non-verbal skills (ie body language), and students who had been working on their assertiveness progressed significantly more if they had good existing non-verbal and verbal skills. In addition, we found that students who had poor self and other awareness struggled with all aspects of the work. From this, we established a hierarchy which forms the basis of the Talkabout resources.

Over the next four years, we piloted this programme using different client groups and a group of willing therapists from throughout the UK. We all found consistently that the success of intervention increased if non-verbal behaviours were taught before verbal behaviours, and if assertiveness was taught last (Kelly, 1996).

This original hierarchy then formed the basis of the first Talkabout book (Kelly, 1996) but it has been adapted over the years to include self-esteem and friendship skills. The hierarchy now looks as follows.

HIERARCHY
Self-awareness and self-esteem
Non-verbal skills
– Body language
– The way we talk
Verbal skills
– Conversational skills
Friendship skills
Assertiveness skills

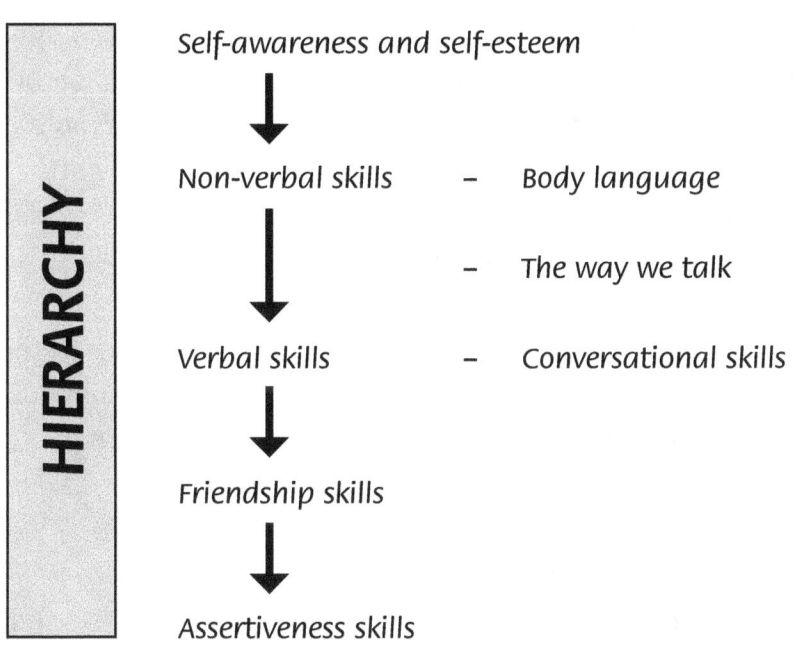

Hierarchy of social skills

So, in planning intervention, we can use this planning tool:

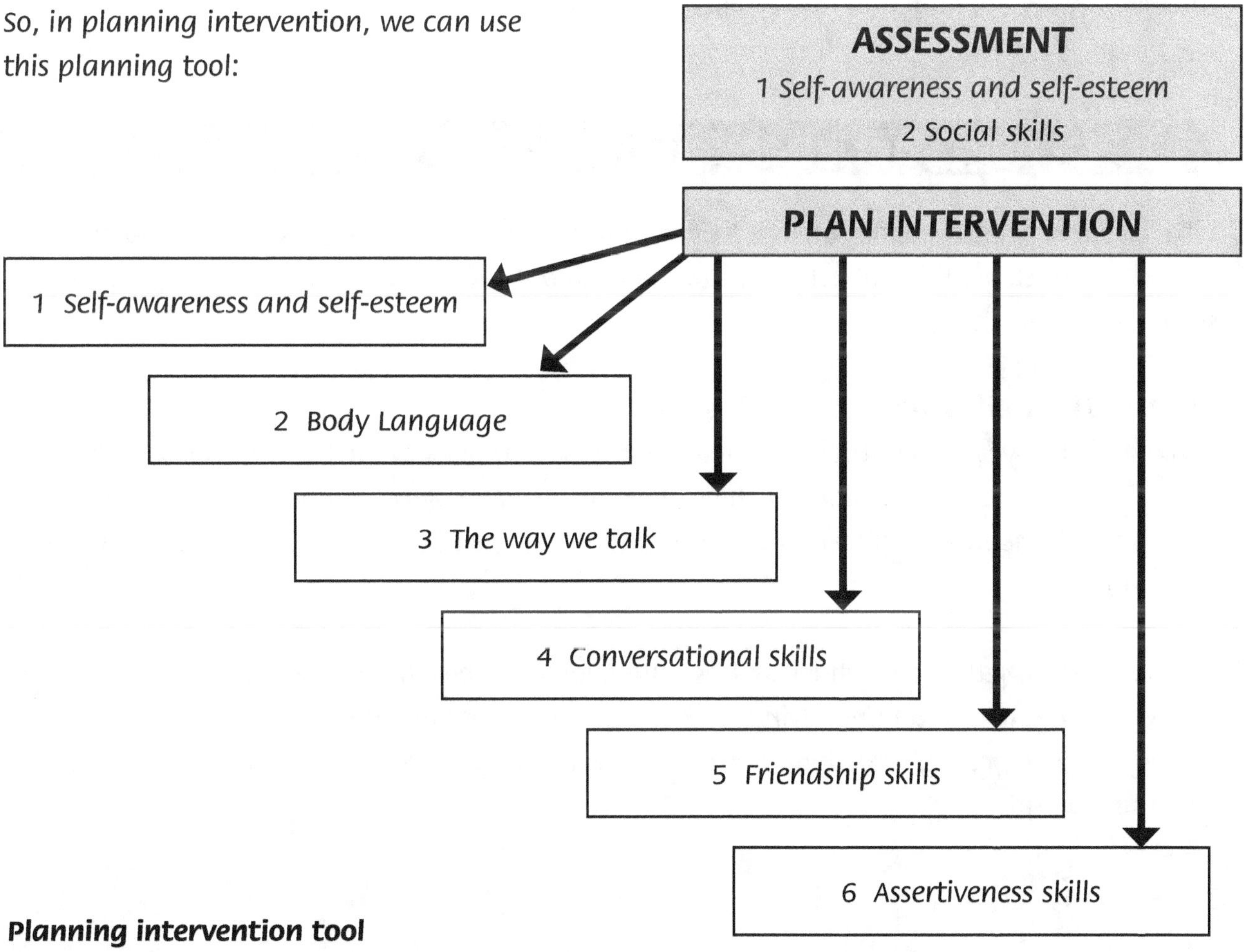

ASSESSMENT
1 Self-awareness and self-esteem
2 Social skills
PLAN INTERVENTION
1 Self-awareness and self-esteem
2 Body Language
3 The way we talk
4 Conversational skills
5 Friendship skills
6 Assertiveness skills

Planning intervention tool

Using this hierarchical approach, teachers and therapists can start work with the person at a level that is appropriate to that person's needs. They can then progress up the levels to enable the person to reach their full potential, ensuring that basic skills are taught before the more complex ones. So a student who needs work on all areas of his social skills would start work first on his body language skills and then would progress to working on his paralinguistic skills, then his conversational skills and, finally, his assertiveness skills.

If this student also had poor self-awareness and low self-esteem, he would need to work on this before working on his social skills. And if a student also had difficulties with his friendship skills, he would only work on developing these skills if he had good self-awareness and good non-verbal and verbal skills.

Of course, success is not just about what you teach first; it is also down to how you teach it. I regularly run training courses in assessing and teaching social skills throughout the UK, and sometimes abroad, so the best way to feel confident about this is to join one of my courses. For more information, please go to my website: **www.alexkelly.biz**

Meanwhile, here are a few of my top tips for making your intervention work.

Planning your intervention

I like to put any intervention into the following four-step plan before I start my group or one-to-one sessions. This will help you to work out how best to work with someone on their social skills difficulties.

Step 1: The behaviour ... what is it?
Make sure that you choose the right behaviour or skill to work on first. So, having assessed the person, you need to consider the hierarchy and the complexity of the skill you want to work on with them. Ask yourself: are you setting up the person to succeed? Is the behaviour too complex?

Now consider whether the behaviour has a function or a reason. Maybe the person is behaving in this way because of an underlying problem that has not been addressed, eg a sensory need. Or they may be getting something out of the behaviour: for example, people leave them alone and they like this.

Finally, try to really describe what the person is doing – the more detailed you can describe the behaviour, the more likely you are to be able to help the person understand what they are doing wrong. You may need to add how it might make other people feel or what they may think to give them insight, although I would do this jointly with the person.

Step 2: The rules ... what are they?
We need to help people to understand what they should be doing instead – what are the rules? What should be happening? So many adults I have worked with have asked me why they were never taught the rules as a child. Of course, before we can do that, we do need to know them ourselves, so that is where I hope the Talkabout resources will help you out!

Step 3: The motivation ... what is it?
Every person you work with will need to be motivated at some level to come to your group, change their behaviour, and become more socially skilled. Often the key to success is to work out what the motivation is going to be for the person to want to change.

We cannot assume that all people are motivated by 'being friendly' or 'friendly behaviour' or 'people will like me' or 'mum will be pleased'. It may be better to reward them with something: for example, an activity, a smiley-face chart or just saying 'This is the polite thing to do' or 'This is the grown-up thing to do'. If we don't consider the motivation, the intervention may fail.

Step 4: The strategy ... which one is best?
There are many different ways of helping people to improve their social skills and usually the best intervention is the one that includes a number of them. There are eight main ways in which we can help someone.

1. **The environment – in the school or at home.** It is essential that the environment backs up what is being taught as much as possible. Think about getting all of the teaching staff on board with what you are working on. Making sure that everyone is encouraging and discouraging in the same way can go a long way to helping someone transfer those skills out of a group and into their everyday life. This doesn't mean I wouldn't work with someone if I can't get the environment to back us up, but it may explain a slower progress. You may see people beginning to get the behaviour in certain situations but not all of them. This is OK. It shows you that the person has the ability to get it right when the environment is conducive.

2. **Talk it through with them or use comic strip conversations.** With many skills and behaviours, it is very helpful to talk it through with the person or to draw it using stick figures and speech bubbles. You will gain an insight into how they may describe what is happening and why it happens, which will help with your intervention.

 **TALKABOUT**

3 **Social story™.** Carol Gray developed this approach in the early 1990s and I often use stories to help teach social skills. A social story gives someone insight into their difficulties and helps them to know what they can do instead. It also contains perspective sentences about what other people may be feeling or thinking which can be very useful for people with ASD.

4 **A visual cue or schedule.** It is important to remember that many people are helped by working visually, so the worksheets and activities in this book will help, but people may also be helped by a prompt card or a poster displayed in the classroom. At our Day Service, 'Speaking Space', in the UK, we use a lot of 'now and next' symbolised strips which can work well to cue people in to what is expected of them in certain situations.

5 **A reward system.** Rewards can help if the motivation is very tangible: for example, stickers to get a financial reward or do an activity, or a certificate of achievement. Other rewards can include a special time with someone to talk about something specific – for example, 20 minutes at the end of the day to talk to their mum about dinosaurs. Any reward needs to work for the person, so you need to refer to their motivation.

6 **Use of other media.** Using DVDs and clips of cartoons or television programmes, or even video clips of you modelling behaviour, can really help to teach social skills. Many people find visual methods of learning much easier and showing a video will usually motivate most people. I often use this method in groups as well as in one-to-one sessions. The Talkabout DVD includes video clips of actors modelling inappropriate and appropriate behaviours for all of the key skills covered in Talkabout (Kelly, 2006).

7 **Role play and modelling.** In this book I often suggest using role play and modelling to help teach skills. Modelling is when the facilitators model a behaviour, both inappropriate and appropriate, and role play is when the group members practise the behaviour themselves.

Here are a few important points to remember when modelling:
- Keep it short and simple.
- Model one behaviour at a time.
- Start with bad behaviour and end with good.
- Never use the group members to help you model behaviours.
- Keep the situation as 'real' as possible – it is better to model a normal conversation between two group facilitators than to pretend that one is a child, shopkeeper or teacher.
- Ask the group what they thought was bad about the behaviour. What should have happened?

Here are a few important points to remember when role playing:
- The group members are asked to act a scenario or to practise a skill.
- It is a stressful experience for some people.
- Try a 'getting into role' exercise such as the magic carpet or twisting into a role like 'Superman'.
- Remember to de-role, especially if the group members have played the part of someone else.
- Consider using puppets.

8. **Social skills group.** This is my favourite way to teach social skills and the Talkabout programme should give you all the resources you need to run a successful social skills group. The advantages of group work over one-to-one work are as follows.
   - It is a more natural and comfortable environment in which to learn.
   - We learn from each other.
   - It is easier to problem solve, play games and to set up role plays.
   - It gives the opportunity to try out new skills in a safe environment.
   - There is an opportunity to transfer skills to other staff, improving the chance of carry-over into the environment.

Setting up and running a Talkabout group

Group membership

It is important to match the group members in terms of both their needs and how well they will get on. A group is far more likely to gel and work well if the participants have similar needs, are a similar age and like each other. Group membership should also be closed, that is, you should not allow new members to join halfway through because this will alter the group dynamics. I like to work with peer groups (children from the same class or year) but it may be more appropriate to choose children from several year groups and classes. If this is the case, I try to have children who are no more than two years apart in age.

Group size

Groups work best if they are neither too small nor too big, preferably between four and eight members. I usually aim for a group of six. You need the group to be small enough to make sure that everyone contributes and feels part of the group and large enough to make activities such as role plays and group discussions feasible and interesting. Even numbers are helpful if sometimes you will ask them to work in pairs.

Group length

Each topic gives you a guideline for the number of sessions it will take to complete but it is important to remember that change will not happen quickly. In terms of the session lengths, it is important that you have enough time to get through your session plan (see the next section) but not so much time that the group members get bored. I usually aim for about 40 minutes.

Group leaders

Groups run better with two leaders (facilitators), especially as there is often a need to model behaviours, observe the group members, video interactions and facilitate group discussions.

Accommodation

You will need a room that is comfortable for the group members to learn in and where you are not going to be interrupted. Don't be tempted to agree to the corner of the hall or library as an acceptable place to run your group – this will not help your group members to relax and talk openly. In terms of the layout of chairs, I sometimes work around a table, depending on the activity; however, it is usually helpful to start with the chairs in a circle for the group cohesion activity.

Cohesiveness

A group that does not gel will not learn or have fun. Therefore, it is important to take time to ensure that the group gels. The factors that help are:

- interpersonal attraction – people who like each other are more likely to gel
- people with similar needs
- activities that encourage everyone to take part and have fun
- arrange the chairs in a circle before the session starts
- ensure that everyone feels valued in the group
- ensure that everyone feels part of the group and has an equal 'say'
- ask the group to set some rules
- start each session with a simple activity that is fun and stress-free
- finish each session with another activity that is fun and stress-free.

Format of the session

The format of the session will vary occasionally but there are some general guidelines which you should follow.

1. **Group cohesion activity**
   This is an essential part of the group. It brings the group together and helps them to focus on the other group members and the purpose of the group. The activity should be simple, stress-free and involve everyone.

2. **How are you feeling?**
   This should be done every session to ensure that the group members learn how to express their feelings and for the facilitator to address any concerns. You will need to use a feelings board from *Talkabout for Adults* (Kelly & Green, 2014) or make up your own version.

3. **Main activity(s)**
   This may include the facilitators modelling a new skill followed by role play by the group members and feedback, and then replay where necessary. It is during this part of the session that it is most important not to lose people's attention by allowing an activity to go on for too long, or one person to dominate the conversation.

4. **Finishing activity**
   Each session should end with a group activity to bring the group members back together again and to reduce anxiety if they have found any of the activities difficult. The activity should therefore be fun, simple and stress-free.

ASSESSMENT

Introduction

Objectives To provide a baseline assessment.

De plan where to start intervention.

Materials
1. Self-awareness and self-esteem interview sheet
2. Social skills assessment sheet
3. Social skills assessment summary
4. Self-assessment rating scale
5. Planning intervention sheet

Timing The timing of the assessment will depend on how well you know the person. If you don't know them well, you may need to talk to a few people and gain their opinions on their social skills and on their self-awareness and self-esteem.

ASSESSMENT

Activity	Description
Self-awareness and self-esteem interview	This initial interview will determine whether the person needs work in this area before you start working on their social skills. This assessment is taken from the *Talkabout for Adults* book (Kelly & Green, 2014).
Social skills assessment	This is a full assessment of the person's social skills. Complete the assessment using a consensus of opinions from other people who know the person well. You can involve the person in the process if appropriate, ie if they can understand the activity but I would usually involve the person in understanding their strengths and needs at the intervention stage (ie when you have already completed your initial assessment). Transfer the assessment to the assessment summary wheel. This assessment wheel is also available to buy on CD Rom (Kelly & Sains, 2010).
Self-assessment sheet	This is an optional part of the assessment process but it can be used to gain information on how much insight the person has into their communication needs. Support the person to complete the self-assessment and score the results.
Planning intervention	Use the information from the 1:1 interview and social skill assessment to plan where to start using the hierarchy: 1 Self-awareness and self-esteem 2 Body language 3 The way we talk 4 Conversational skills 5 Assertiveness

ASSESSMENT

Assessment of self-awareness and self-esteem

Name …………………………………………….. DOB …………………….

Address …………………………………………….. Date …………………….

Use the questions below to help find out whether the person has good self-awareness and self-esteem. You could use pictures and other forms of stimuli to elicit answers if appropriate.

---

1 Tell me about a good friend

Why do you like them? What do they look like? What are they like? (Other awareness)

---

2 Why do you think your friend likes you?

(Qualities and self-esteem)

---

3 Tell me about you. What do you like doing?

Do you have a favourite hobby or activity? (Likes)

---

4 Is there anything you really don't like doing?

(Dislikes)

(continued)

ASSESSMENT

5 What do you think you are good at?

Can you think of something that you are good at? (Strengths and self-esteem)

6 Can you think of something that you find difficult?

Can you think of something that you are not so good at? (Needs and self-esteem)

7 How would you describe the way you look?

Can you tell me 3 things about the way you look? (Personal appearance and self-esteem)

8 What kind of person do you think you are?

Can you think of 3 words to describe what kind of person you are? (Qualities and self-esteem)

9 Can you think of one good thing about being you?

Is there something that makes you special or really happy? (Qualities and self-esteem)

10 Do you like talking to people?

Do you find it easy or difficult to talk to people? (Strengths and self-esteem)

ASSESSMENT

Summary

1	Able to tell you what they look like? (Personal appearance)	Yes	No
2	Able to describe a friend or another person? (Other awareness)	Yes	No
3	Able to say what they like and dislike? (Likes, dislikes)	Yes	No
4	Able to give you two qualities about self? (Strengths, needs, qualities)	Yes	No
5	Appears to have good self-esteem? (Self esteem)	Yes	No

Comments

Completed by .... Date ....

ASSESSMENT

Social Skills Assessment

Name .... DOB ....

Address .... Date ....

Rating scale and symbols:

1	2	3	4
Never good	Not Very good	Quite good	Very good
☹	☹	☺	☺

Complete the assessment below using a consensus of opinions from other people who know the person well.

Transfer the assessment below to the assessment summary wheel.

Body Language					
	1	2	3	4	
Eye contact Never good – avoids eye contact at all times during conversations or continuously stares					Very good – effective and appropriate use of eye contact in all situations
Facial expression Never good – inappropriate to situation. May include scowling, grinning, blank expression, etc.					Very good – effective use of a range of facial expressions, changing according to the situation, eg expresses own moods and feelings through facial expressions
Gestures Never good – uses inappropriate hand gestures excessively, or no use of hand gestures					Very good – uses hand gestures effectively, eg for emphasis or substitution of speech
Distance Never good – inappropriate distance when communicating, causing discomfort to others					Very good – adapts distance appropriately and effectively, ie according to relationships and social situations
Touch Never good – excessive use or avoidance of touch which causes embarrassment or anger in others					Very good – effective and appropriate use of touch, ie a degree of touch which is acceptable to others and/or the situation

ASSESSMENT

Body Language (continued)

	1	2	3	4	
Fidgeting Never good – excessive fidgeting that is distracting and causes a barrier to communication					Very good – rarely fidgets
Posture Never good – usually inappropriate to situation, ie inappropriately rigid or relaxed					Very good – normal posture and gait, appropriate to all situations
Personal appearance Never good – habitually unkempt appearance and/or inappropriate clothing for season or situation					Very good – maintains and adapts appearance to different situations, seasons and age. Uses appearance to create different impressions

The Way We Talk

	1	2	3	4	
Volume Never good – mostly uses inappropriate volume, eg voice too loud or quiet for the situation					Very good – uses and adapts volume appropriately in all situations
Rate Never good – consistently inappropriate rate, eg too fast, slow, fluctuating between extremes					Very good – rate of speech is appropriate and adapted effectively, eg increasing rate when there is a sense of urgency
Clarity Never good – habitual use of indistinct speech, eg mumbling					Very good – speech is consistently clear and easily understood
Intonation Never good – consistently inappropriate, eg monotonous or exaggerated					Very good – intonation is used effectively and appropriately, ie adapted to situation and content of speech
Fluency Never good – consistently dysfluent, eg severe hesitations in speech, excessive use of 'um' and 'er'					Very good – fluent speech

ASSESSMENT

Conversational Skills

	1	2	3	4	
Listening Never good – difficulty in listening and lack of non-verbal reinforcement, eg. eye contact, nodding					Very good – a good listener showing effective and appropriate use of non-verbal reinforcers
Starting a conversation Never good – rarely initiates conversations or inappropriate to situation, eg habitual subject matter					Very good – effective and appropriate use of conversation starters
Taking turns Never good – monopolises conversations with minimal listening or makes few contributions					Very good – uses good turn-taking skills and effectively responds to cues, eg natural breaks, eye contact, questioning
Asking questions Never good – does not ask questions during conversations or seek further information when needed					Very good – asks questions with appropriate frequency especially when gaining information to maintain a conversation
Answering questions Never good – does not answer questions during conversations or uses minimal utterances, eg 'yes', 'no'					Very good – responds to questions effectively and appropriately to maintain a conversation
Being relevant Never good – has difficulty in following a topic of conversation, eg introduces unrelated ideas					Very good – can maintain and develop a topic effectively and appropriately
Repairing Never good – does not seek clarification or further information when a misunderstanding occurs					Very good – seeks clarification and further information effectively and appropriately
Ending a conversation Never good – has great difficulty in ending conversations or goes off without adequate closure					Very good – consistently ends conversations effectively and appropriately with appropriate non-verbal and verbal behaviour

ASSESSMENT

Assertiveness Skills					
	1	2	3	4	
Expressing feelings Never good – does not express feelings or needs effectively or appropriately. May appear passive or aggressive in their ability to tell you how they feel					Very good – effective and appropriate expression of feelings or needs, ie expresses feelings with appropriate body language and vocabulary
Standing up for yourself Never good – does not stand up for self or rights and may appear passive or aggressive or will stand up for self inappropriately					Very good – stands up for self or rights effectively and appropriately, ie can represent own views and feelings in an assertive way
Making suggestions Never good – does not make suggestions. May appear passive, easily led, or continuously making suggestions, or not listening to others					Very good – makes suggestions or gives opinions effectively and appropriately and in the correct context
Refusing Never good – always complies with requests even when against their will or will refuse aggressively, inappropriately or continuously					Very good – has well-developed skills in refusal which are used effectively and appropriately, ie uses appropriate non-verbal and verbal behaviour
Disagreeing Never good – does not disagree with opinions and may appear passive or easily influenced or will disagree aggressively or continuously					Very good – disagrees with opinions and statements effectively and appropriately, ie uses good non-verbal and verbal behaviour
Complaining Never good – does not complain when appropriate or may communicate dissatisfaction inappropriately and complain continuously					Very good – complains effectively and appropriately to the situation by stating reasons clearly and assertively
Apologising Never good – does not apologise when appropriate or expected, may be defensive or aggressive or continuously apologises inappropriately					Very good – apologises effectively and appropriately using appropriate verbal and non-verbal behaviour
Requesting explanations Never good – does not question requests or decisions and may respond inappropriately or continuously requests inappropriately					Very good – shows effective skills in requesting further explanations when necessary

# ASSESSMENT

Comments

Completed by .... Date ....

ASSESSMENT

Social Skills Assessment Summary

Name .... Date ....

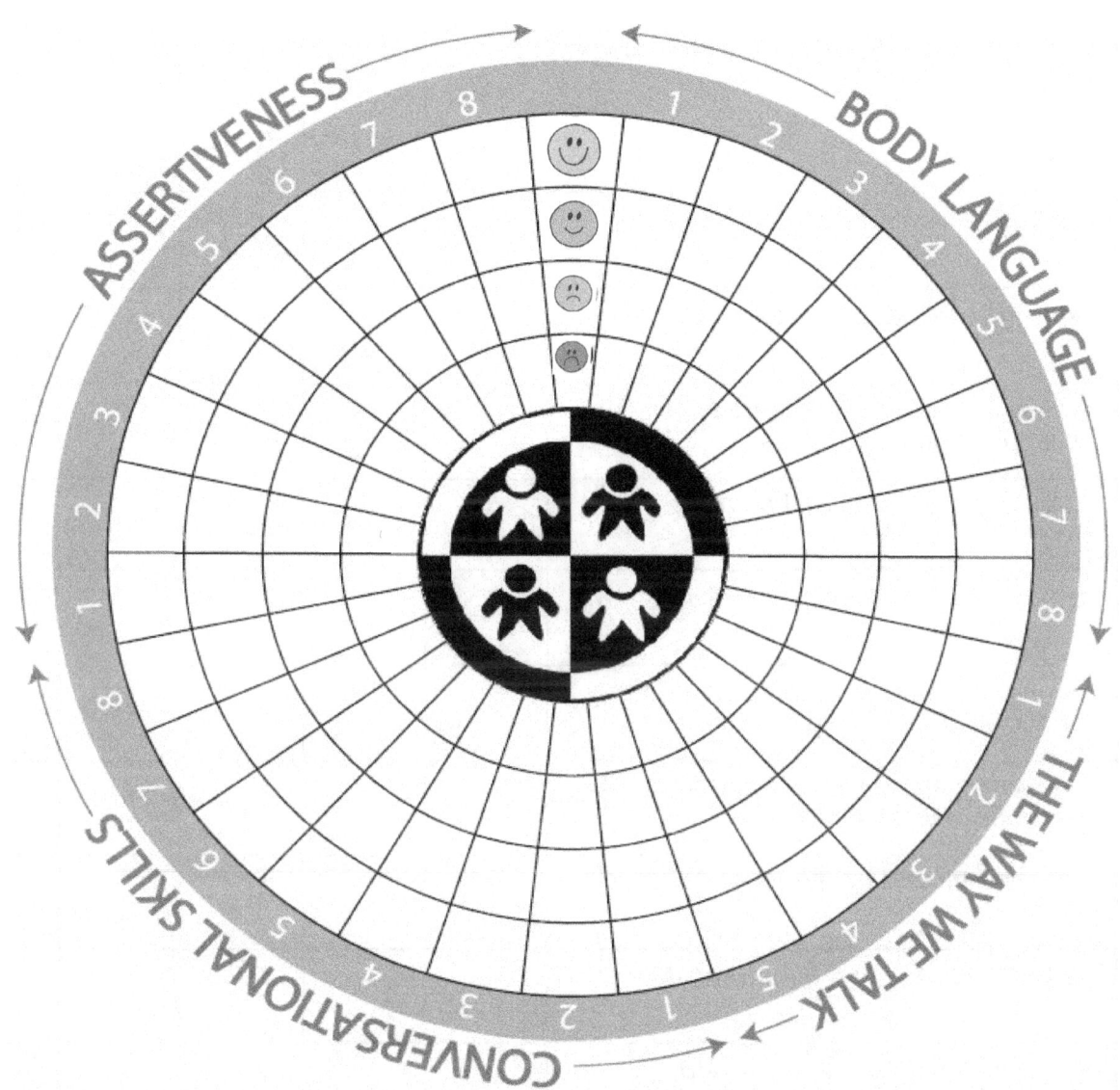

BODY LANGUAGE	THE WAY WE TALK	CONVERSATIONAL SKILLS	ASSERTIVENESS
1 Eye contact 2 Facial expression 3 Gesture 4 Distance 5 Touch 6 Fidgeting 7 Posture 8 Personal appearance	1 Volume 2 Rate 3 Clarity 4 Intonation 5 Fluency	1 Listening 2 Starting a conversation 3 Taking turns 4 Asking questions 5 Answering questions 6 Being relevant 7 Repairing 8 Ending a conversation	1 Expressing feelings 2 Standing up for self 3 Making suggestions 4 Refusing 5 Disagreeing 6 Complaining 7 Apologising 8 Requesting explanation

ASSESSMENT

Self-Assessment Rating Scale

Your name .... Date ....

What are you like at the following?	Never good	Not very good	Quite good	Very good	I don't know
1 Talking to a friend when we are on our own					
2 Talking to friends in a group					
3 Talking to someone in authority, for example a policeman, a boss					
4 Talking to new people who I meet					
5 Listening to people who are talking to me					
6 Asking questions, for example if I don't understand something					
7 Answering questions, for example if someone asks me directions					
8 Keeping still and not fidgeting too much					
9 Speaking clearly and not mumbling					
10 Explaining something to a group of people, for example in a meeting					

Any other comments you would like to make about your communication?

Total score: .... / 40

(Rating scale: Never good = 1   Not very good = 2   Quite good = 3   Very good = 4   I don't know = 0)

Completed by .... Date ....

ASSESSMENT

Planning Intervention Sheet

Name .... DOB ....

Address .... Date ....

Area assessed	Needs work?	Start here
Self-awareness and self-esteem Refer to interview	No / Yes	**Self-awareness and self-esteem** Use *Talkabout for Adults* book (2014)
Body Language Refer to social skills assessment	No / Yes	**Body Language** Use Level 1 Talkabout Body Language
The Way We Talk Refer to social skills assessment	No / Yes	**The Way We Talk** Use Level 2 Talkabout The Way We Talk
Conversational Skills Refer to social skills assessment	No / Yes	**Conversations** Use Level 3 Talkabout Conversations
Assertiveness Skills Refer to social skills assessment	No / Yes	**Assertiveness** Use Level 4 Talkabout Assertiveness

Additional comments

Completed by .... Date ....

ASSESSMENT

Level 1 Talkabout Body Language

Introduction

Objectives To introduce the concept of body language.

To introduce the eight aspects of body language:

- eye contact
- facial expression
- gesture
- distance
- touch
- fidgeting
- posture
- personal appearance.

Materials You will need to photocopy some of the activities.

Some of the activity worksheets are best enlarged to A3 size.

Some of the activity cards are best laminated so that you can use them again.

Some activities are designed to be A5 size to create a 'fact book' of social skills.

Timing The topics in Level 1 will take up to 46 sessions to complete.

TALKABOUT Body Language

Contents — page

Topic 1 — Talkabout body language

Activity 1	Watch us talk!	36
Activity 2	Watch that man	38
Activity 3	What is body language?	39
Activity 4	In the manner of the word	43
Activity 5	What happens to our bodies when …?	46
Activity 6	Body language … what am I like? (part 1)	50

Topic 2 — Eye contact

Activity 7	Watch my eyes!	53
Activity 8	Blindfold game	56
Activity 9	Why is eye contact important?	57
Activity 10	The rules for eye contact	61
Activity 11	Learning to look	64
Activity 12	Stop and look	66

Topic 3 — Facial expression

Activity 13	Watch my face!	67
Activity 14	Why is facial expression important?	69
Activity 15	Different feelings	71
Activity 16	The rules for facial expression	74
Activity 17	Face your emotions	76

Topic 4 — Gesture

Activity 18	Watch my hands!	77
Activity 19	Why is gesture important?	79
Activity 20	Different gestures	81
Activity 21	The rules for gesture	83
Activity 22	Give us a hand	85

Topic 5 — Distance

Activity 23	Watch the distance!	87
Activity 24	That's a close one!	89
Activity 25	Closer to you?	90
Activity 26	The rules for distance	92
Activity 27	Mind the gap!	94

TALKABOUT Body Language

Topic 6	**Touch**	
Activity 28	Watch my touch!	95
Activity 29	Touch control	97
Activity 30	Why is touch important?	101
Activity 31	The rules for touch	103
Activity 32	To touch or not to touch?	105

Topic 7	**Fidgeting**	
Activity 33	Watch me fidget!	107
Activity 34	Why do people fidget?	109
Activity 35	The rules for fidgeting	111

Topic 8	**Posture**	
Activity 36	Watch my posture!	113
Activity 37	Walk this way	115
Activity 38	Posture thermometer	116
Activity 39	Different postures	118
Activity 40	The rules for posture	119
Activity 41	Time to pose!	121

Topic 9	**Personal appearance**	
Activity 42	Watch my appearance!	122
Activity 43	Looking good!	124
Activity 44	The rules for personal appearance	126
Activity 45	Dressed to impress	128

Topic 10	**My body language … how did I do?**	
Activity 46	Body language … What am I like? (part 2)	130

TALKABOUT Body Language

Topic 1 Talkabout body language

Activity 1 Watch us talk!

Preparation

You will need a large sheet of paper and pens to write down discussion ideas.

Photocopies of the handout.

You may want to prepare short role plays (modelling) of you and a co-facilitator having a conversation or source a few video clips of people talking to each other. You could use a couple of clips from the Talkabout DVD.

Instructions

- Ask the group to think about the different ways in which we communicate.

- You could role play a model conversation or show video clips of people talking, to get the group talking to each other in different ways.

- Write up all the ideas on a large piece of paper. Support the group to begin thinking in terms of body language, the way we talk and having conversations.

- Then ask the group members to look at the cartoon on the handout. What do they notice about how the people are communicating?

- Introduce the main three ways we communicate and what they mean, including any ideas the group have thought of.

- Explain to the group that they will now be focusing on the skills of body language in this session.

TALKABOUT Body Language

Activity 1 'Watch us talk!' handout

How do we communicate?

Have a look at the cartoon below. How are they communicating with each other?

Through ...

1. BODY LANGUAGE

2. THE WAY WE SAY THINGS

3. HAVING CONVERSATIONS

TALKABOUT Body Language

Activity 2 Watch that man

Preparation

You will need some large sheets of paper and pens to write down discussion ideas.

Find short video clips from popular television programmes that show different aspects of body language: eye contact, facial expression, gesture, distance, touch, fidgeting, posture and personal appearance. The soaps can work well or use the introduction to body language clips on the Talkabout DVD.

Instructions

- Explain to the group that they are going to watch some video clips with the sound off.

- Get the group to watch the clips and think about what the actors are doing with their bodies to communicate with each other.

- Discuss as a group what they noticed and use their responses to help the group members identify the eight aspects of body language:

    o eye contact

    o facial expression

    o gesture

    o distance

    o touch

    o fidgeting

    o posture

    o personal appearance.

TALKABOUT Body Language

Activity 3 What is body language?

Preparation

Photocopy the 'What is body language?' board and the cards. Laminate the board and cards if you want to use them again. You could also add a small piece of Velcro™ to the back of each card with a corresponding piece on each square of the brainstorm board.

Instructions

- Ask the group if they can remember any of t   eight aspects of body language; add these cards to the board if people say them.

- You may like to watch again one of the body language video clips from the previous activity to help remind group members of the part of body language.

- As the group members say each one, discuss how we use it to communicate. What does it show us?

- Continue until you have spoken about all aspects and added them to the board.

- You can then give each group member the summary handout to add to their workbook of social skills if they are completing one.

Variation

Put all the cards in a bag or in a pile face-down in the middle of the group. Group members take it in turns to pick a card and then tell the group how that body part can be used to communicate. The group then discuss the question: does everyone agree?

TALKABOUT Body Language

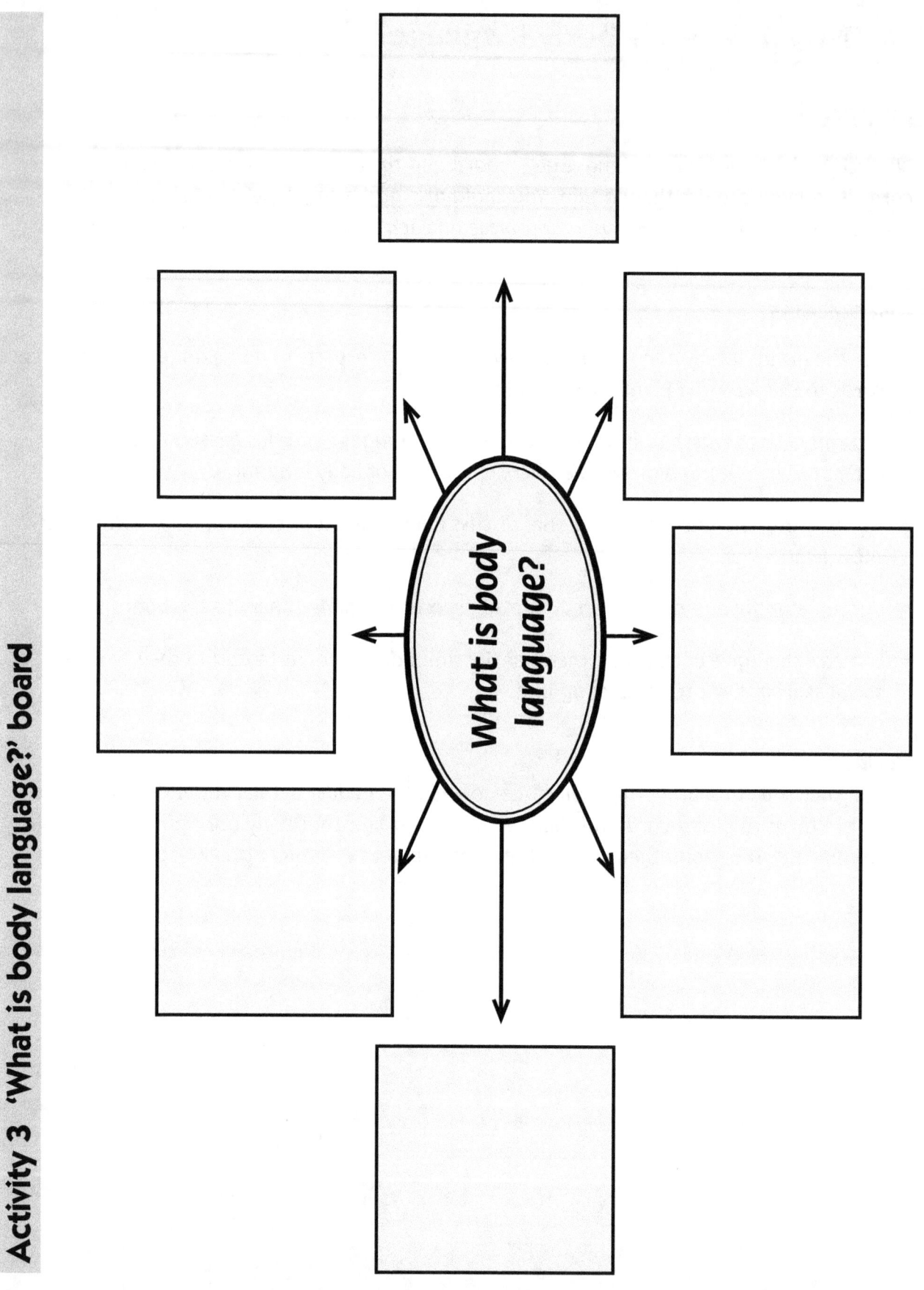

Activity 3 'What is body language?' board

TALKABOUT Body Language

Activity 3 'What is body language?' cards

eye contact

facial expression

gesture

distance

touch

fidgeting

posture

personal appearance

TALKABOUT Body Language

Activity 3 'What is body language?' summary

Name .... Date ....

What is body language?

- gesture
- distance
- touch
- fidgeting
- posture
- personal appearance
- eye contact
- facial expression

TALKABOUT Body Language

Activity 4 In the manner of the word

Preparation

Photocopy the action cards and laminate them if you want to use them again.

You will also need a wipe board or large piece of paper and a pen.

Instructions

- Ask the group to think of as many emotions as they can. The group facilitator then writes them up on the wipe board or piece of paper.

- Group members take it in turns to pick up an activity card and choose an emotion from the list. They must not tell anyone what these are.

- The group member then performs the action 'in the manner of the word', for example brushes their teeth angrily, or watches television scared.

- The rest of the group watch and then try to guess what the person is doing and, most importantly, which emotion they are expressing.

- Once the group members have guessed, they discuss what changed about the person's body to show that emotion.

- The next group member then has a turn. The game continues until everyone has had a chance to perform. The action cards can be used more than once.

Variation
If the group members don't like to perform alone, they can be put in pairs or divided into two teams and collect points for correctly guessed actions. The team with the most points at the end wins.

TALKABOUT Body Language

Activity 4 'In the manner of the word' cards

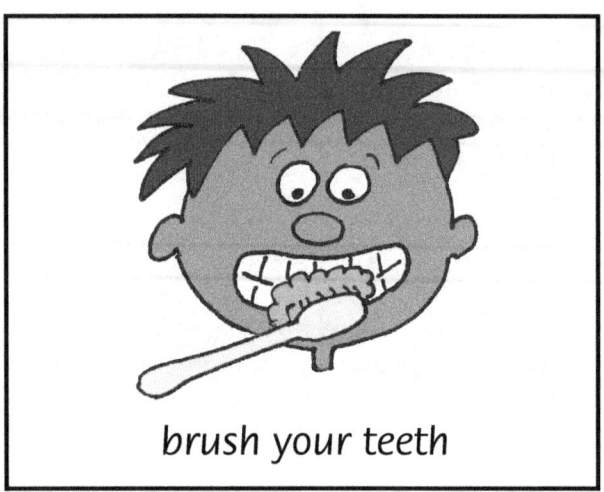
brush your teeth

get dressed

watch television

wash your hair

pack your bag

make breakfast

Activity 4 'In the manner of the word' cards (continued)

read a book

draw a picture

sweep the floor

do the washing-up

eat your dinner

make a cup of tea

TALKABOUT Body Language

Activity 5 What happens to our bodies when …?

Preparation

Photocopy the cards and stick the title cards back-to-back with the corresponding information cards. Laminate these if you want to use them again.

Photocopy the worksheet. You may like to enlarge this to A3 size if you are completing this activity as a group and have a few copies, one for each emotion you talk about.

Instructions

- Explain to the group that they are going to be thinking about different emotions and what effect these have on our body language.

- Choose an emotion to begin with, such as anger. Turn over the first card – 'face' – and, as a group, decide which description fits best for when we are angry. It may help to get all of the group to pretend to be angry and then have a look round at each other's faces. The group facilitator then writes this description on the worksheet.

- The group can add other descriptions if they like.

- Move on to the next area – 'eyes' – and continue until they have completed the sheet for that emotion.

- The group can then complete a sheet about another emotion, eg sad or happy.

Variation

You could just complete this activity as a discussion. Choose an emotion and get each group member to turn over a card and say how that part of the body changes when they feel the chosen emotion.

Alternatively, you could pair up group members and give each pair an emotion to complete a worksheet on. They would then regroup at the end of the session and share their ideas.

TALKABOUT Body Language

Activity 5 'What happens to our bodies when ...?' cards

face

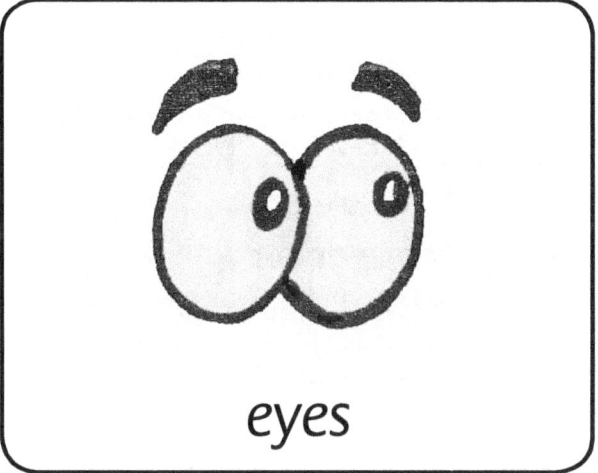
eyes

hands

distance

posture

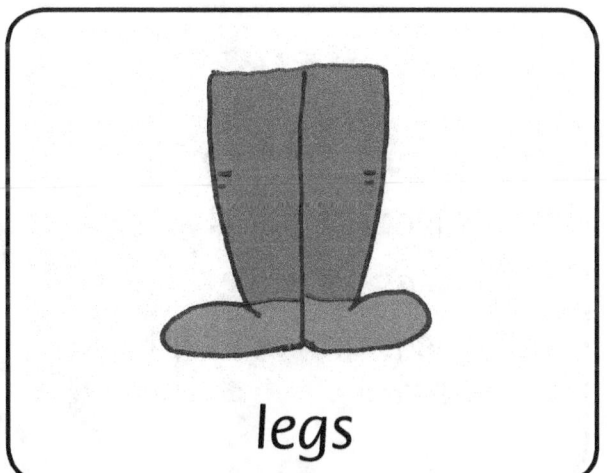
legs

TALKABOUT Body Language

Activity 5 'What happens to our bodies when …?' information cards

Eyes

- Eyes are wide open
- Eyes are raised
- Eyes are down
- Eyes are looking around
- Eyes are relaxed

Face

- My cheeks are burning
- My face is sweaty
- My face is pale
- My face is a normal colour

Distance

- I want to run away
- I want to hug someone
- I get close to someone
- My distance is normal

Hands

- Fists are clenched
- Hands are sweaty
- Hands are fidgety
- Gesturing a lot
- Hands feel relaxed

Legs

- My knees are trembling
- My feet are fidgety
- My legs are stiff
- My legs are nice and relaxed

Posture

- My body is tense
- My body is relaxed
- My body is slouched
- I have good posture

TALKABOUT Body Language

Activity 5 'What happens to our bodies when …?' worksheet

Name ……………………………………………………….. Date ……………………

When I feel ………………… this is what happens to my body …

	Face	
	Eyes	
	Hands	
	Distance	
	Posture	
	Legs	

I may also …

49

TALKABOUT Body Language

Activity 6 Body language ... What am I like? (part 1)

Preparation

Photocopy the worksheet, one for each group member. You may like to enlarge one to A3 size to use in group discussion.

Photocopy a target sheet for each group member.

Instructions

- Remind the group that they will be focusing on body language for the next few weeks. Therefore, they are going to plan today what they need to work on.

- As a group, go through the 'What am I like at body language?' worksheet, explaining the different behaviours and the rating scale. It is a good idea to get the group used to the rating scale first by rating different skills such as cooking, cycling, getting out of bed in the morning.

- Then ask the group members to rate where they think they are with their body language behaviours. They may prefer to sit quietly in a corner of the room to complete this task.

- The group facilitator takes it in turns to sit with each group member individually to talk through how they have rated themselves. The facilitator can then share how they rated that group member on their Talkabout assessment summary wheel (page 29 , only the body language section), raising awareness of what they need to improve on and what they are already doing well.

- The group members can then complete a target sheet for the body language topic.

TALKABOUT Body Language

Activity 6 'What am I like at body language?' worksheet

Name .... Date ....

Body language ... what am I like at it?

	Never good	Not very good	Quite good	Very good
❶ Eye contact				
❷ Facial expression				
❸ Gesture				
❹ Distance				
❺ Touch				
❻ Fidgeting				
❼ Posture				
❽ Personal appearance				

TALKABOUT Body Language

Activity 6 'What am I like at body language?' target sheet

Name ………………………………………………………… Date ……………………

My Body Language Plan

 I am good at …

I need to work on …

How did I get on?

TALKABOUT Body Language ... Eye contact

Topic 2 Eye contact

Activity 7 Watch my eyes!

Preparation

You may need large sheets of paper and pens to write down discussion ideas.

Photocopies of the worksheets.

You may want to prepare short role plays (modelling) of you and a co-facilitator having a conversation or source a few video clips of people talking to each other. You could use the eye contact clips on the Talkabout DVD as an alternative to the modelling.

Instructions

- Ask the group to watch you and your co-facilitator have a conversation. Use a normal scenario, for example talking to each other about what you did at the weekend. In the first scenario, one of the group facilitators should use no eye contact while the other person talks normally. Stop and ask the group what they noticed. Was there anything that was not good? They will probably say either the person wasn't listening or they were not looking. In each case, you can ask them what should have happened and they will say you should have looked at the other person. You then suggest that you will do better the next time.

- In the second role play, one of you should stare very obviously without changing your posture too much. You may need to open your eyes very wide and use slightly exaggerated facial expressions to cue them into your eye contact being inappropriate. Stop and ask the group what they noticed. Was there anything that was not good? You can then talk about eye contact that is too much and that we don't like people who stare. Talk about how much we should look and suggest that you will try to do better the next time.

- In the third role play, you can use appropriate eye contact.

- At each point, talk about how it makes people appear if they stare or use no eye contact. Use the phrases on the first worksheet to help.

- The group members can then complete the summary worksheet.

TALKABOUT Body Language ... Eye contact

Activity 7 'Watch my eyes!' worksheet 1

Name .... Date ....

Poor communication

What do people think?

They are strange	They are not listening
They are not nice	They are bored
They are not friendly	They are not interested
They are shy	They are rude
They are nervous	They are not confident

How do people feel?

Nervous	Embarrassed
Worried	Irritated
Sad	Angry
Bored	Shy
Confused	Uncomfortable

54

TALKABOUT Body Language ... Eye contact

Activity 7 'Watch my eyes!' worksheet 2

Name .... Date ....

Poor eye contact

❶ Looking away ...

This means we may look around the room or at something else when we are talking to someone.

If we look away when we are talking to someone:

The other person may think ....

The other person may feel ....

❷ Staring ...

This means we may look at someone's eyes too much when we are talking to them.

If we stare when we are talking to someone:

The other person may think ....

The other person may feel ....

TALKABOUT Body Language ... Eye contact

Activity 8 Blindfold game

Preparation

You can use scarves or blindfolds for this activity to help the group members to keep their eyes closed. Alternatively, you can just ask them to close their eyes.

Instructions

- Explain to the group that they are going to sit in a circle and have a conversation. It may help to give them a topic, such as what they are doing at the weekend, or to talk about their favourite holiday.

- Explain that they are going to have the whole conversation with their eyes closed or blindfolded. You may want to agree a time limit, such as two minutes.

- At the end of the time, ask them what was difficult about the conversation:
  o Starting it?
  o Showing interest or listening?
  o Taking turns?
  o Knowing whether people were interested or bored?
  o Something else?

- Discuss why eye contact or looking at each other would make the conversation easier.

- You could repeat the conversation without the blindfolds if you feel it would be helpful.

Variation

You could ask two group members to sit back-to-back and have a conversation.

TALKABOUT Body Language ... Eye contact

Activity 9 Why is eye contact important?

Preparation

Photocopy the cards and stick them back-to-back. Laminate them if you want to use them again.

Photocopies of the worksheet.

Instructions

- Explain to the group that you are going to think about all the reasons why and when eye contact is important. For example:

    o To help start a conversation – we use more eye contact at the beginning of a conversation.

    o To show people we are listening – we need to use more eye contact when we are listening than when we are talking.

    o To show interest – we look at people to let them know we are interested in what they are saying. We widen our eyes to show real interest.

    o To watch the other person to see how they are feeling – we look at their eyes to see if they are looking at us (good sign!) or looking around the room (not a good sign!). We can also look at their facial expression.

    o To take turns – we use more eye contact as we hand over the conversation to the other person.

    o To be polite – people like people who use good eye contact.

- You could demonstrate these through different role plays (modelling) or you could use the cards to get a discussion going. If you are using the cards, put them text-side down. You could start by asking what they think the pictures mean and then take it in turns to pick them up and discuss what is written on the other side.

- The group members can then complete their worksheet.

TALKABOUT Body Language ... Eye contact

Activity 9 'Why is eye contact important?' cards

To help start a conversation

We use more eye contact at the beginning of a conversation.

To show we are interested

We look at people to let them know we are interested in what they are saying. We widen our eyes to show real interest.

To take turns

We use more eye contact as we hand over the conversation to the other person.

TALKABOUT Body Language ... Eye contact

Activity 9 'Why is eye contact important?' cards (continued)

To show we are listening

We need to use more eye contact when we are listening than when we are talking.

To see how the other person is feeling

We look at their eyes to see if they are looking at us (good sign!) or looking around the room (not a good sign!). We can also look at their facial expression.

To be polite

People like talking to people who use good eye contact.

TALKABOUT Body Language ... Eye contact

Activity 9 'Why is eye contact important?' worksheet

Name .... Date ....

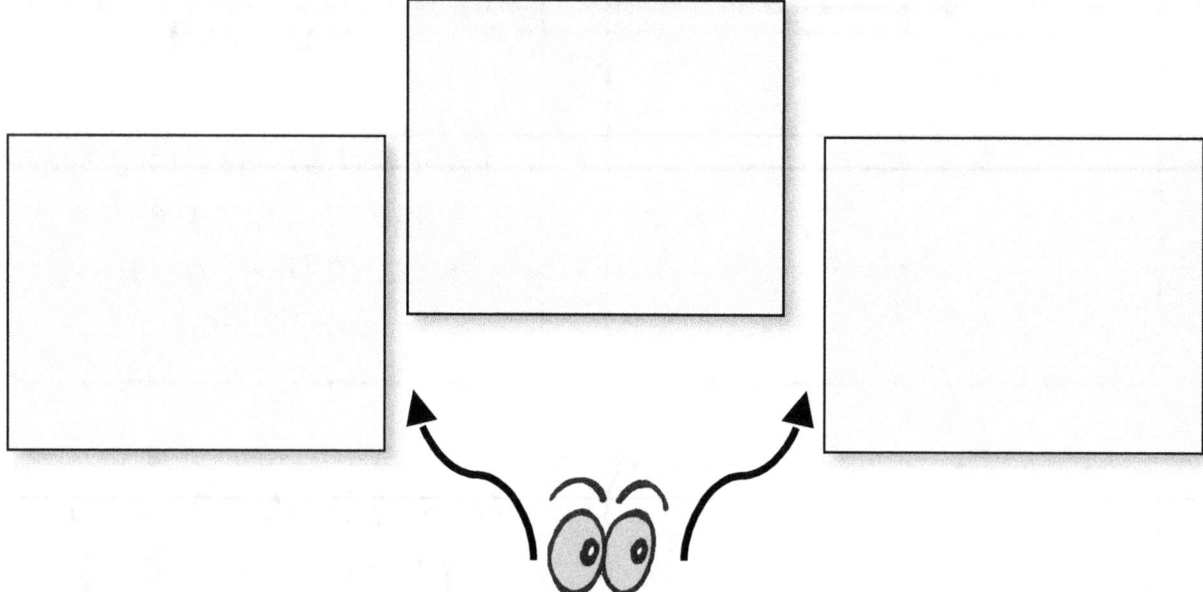

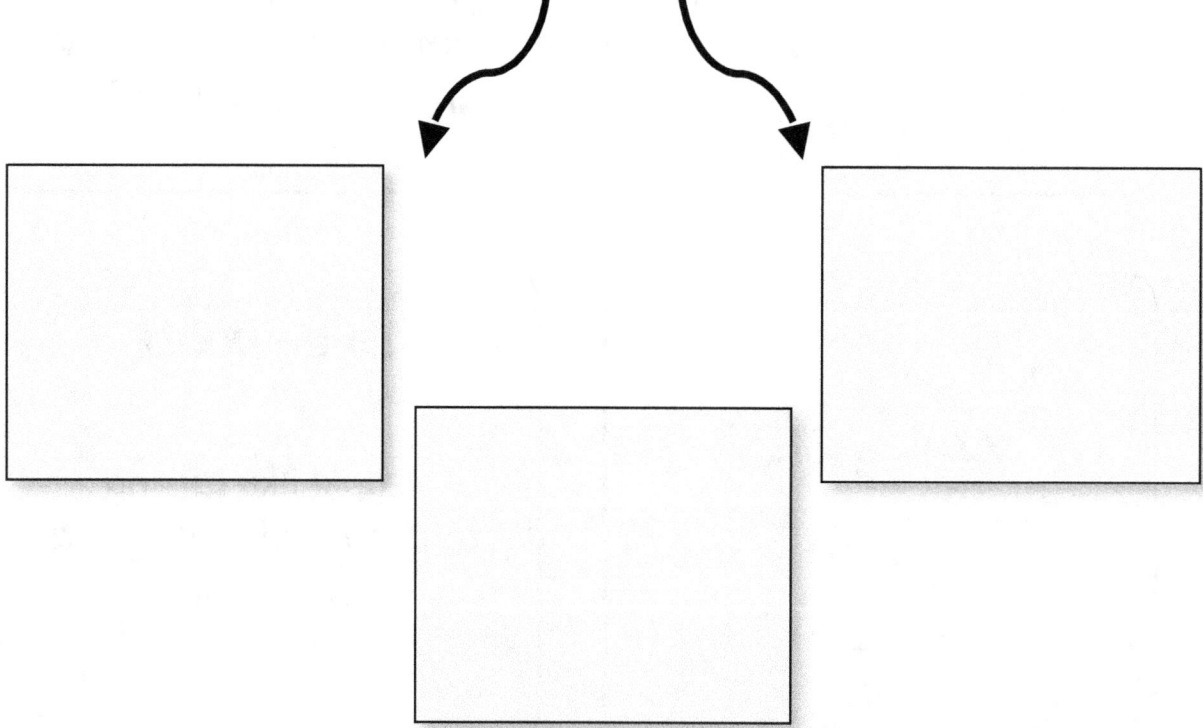

TALKABOUT Body Language ... Eye contact

Activity 10 The rules for eye contact

Preparation

Photocopy the worksheet and the handout. Cut them to size if the group members are going to put these in their A5 fact book.

It may help to have a see-through triangle that can be placed on a drawn face on the wipe board or can be placed in front of their faces.

Instructions

- Explain to the group that you are going to work out the rule for good eye contact.

- Ask the group to agree where it is good to look in the face. You could draw a face on a wipe board and then use a triangle to agree where in the face it is OK to look. Ask the group to position it in different places and then you could demonstrate this with your co-facilitator.

    o You are aiming for it to be across the eyebrows and then down to the end of the nose.

- Talk about why it may be not OK to look at someone's mouth.

    o It is more intimate and can be seen as a flirting behaviour.

- Ask the group to identify where in the triangle they would feel OK looking at. If they find it hard to look at someone's eyes, ask them to consider in between the eyes or the bridge of the nose.

- The group members could then practise looking at each other using the triangle rule. You can use stickers on your face or bridge of nose, for example, if that helps them to cue in to where they should be looking.

TALKABOUT Body Language ... Eye contact

Activity 10 'The rules of eye contact' worksheet

Name .... Date ....

Can you draw a triangle ▽ on the face to show where you can look when you are talking to someone?

Sometimes we may briefly look at someone's mouth when we are talking to them. What do you think that means?

TALKABOUT Body Language ... Eye contact

Activity 10 'The rules for eye contact' handout

Name .... Date ....

Eye contact

What is good eye contact?

✓ Good eye contact means we should look towards the person who is talking to us

✓ If you can look at the person's eyes then great

✓ If it is difficult to look at their eyes, look at them somewhere in the triangle

✓ It is OK to look away for a few seconds – we do not want to stare

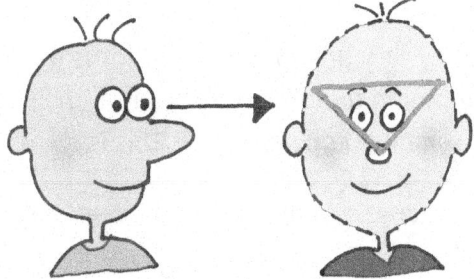

! Why is this important?

It is polite to look at people when we are talking to them. We need to show people we are listening to them. We can also use it to see how the other person is feeling and to help us take turns. Eye contact is more important at the beginning of the conversation and when we are listening rather than speaking.

If we don't use good eye contact, people may also think we are rude and not want to talk to us.

TALKABOUT Body Language ... Eye contact

Activity 11 Learning to look

Preparation

Photocopy the worksheet and cut them to size if the group members are going to put them in their A5 fact book.

Note: you will use this worksheet again for future topics and skills.

Instructions

- Explain to the group that you are going to think about what everyone can do to help them to use good eye contact.

- First, ask them to think about what they are currently doing wrong. Are they looking away too much? Help everyone to describe it by starting the sentence 'Sometimes I ...'

- Then think about what other people may think or feel about them using poor eye contact. Finish the sentence 'Other people may think ...'

- Then ask them to think of a sentence that will help them to remember the rule or what they will do. Finish the sentence 'I will try to ...'

- Finally, think about why they are doing this. What is the motivation? Is it good to do this because it is the polite thing to do? Or is it because their parents will be proud? Or do they need a reward? This sentence can start with 'This is ...' or 'This will mean that ...'

- If they would like a written reminder of this for their fact book, complete the worksheet and cut it to size.

TALKABOUT Body Language ... Eye contact

Activity 11 'Learning to look' worksheet

Name .... Date ....

I am working on my ...

Sometimes I ....

....

....

Other people may think ....

....

I will try to ....

....

This ....

....

My name .... Date ....

Activity 12 Stop and look

Preparation

Create some space in the room so that the group members can move around freely.

You may like to set up a way to play music for this activity; you will need to be able to stop and start it easily.

You may also like to have a video recording device ready to record group members' good eye contact.

Instructions

- Explain to the group that you are going to move around the room and when the music stops, or the facilitator says 'Stop', they turn to the person nearest to them. They will then try to use their good eye contact while each person asks a question.

- You can make this simpler by agreeing a few questions beforehand, for example:
    o What is your favourite colour?
    o What did you do at the weekend?
    o What do you like to do in the evenings?
    o What is your favourite meal?

- The group facilitator watches the group and encourages some of the pairs to show the others their good eye contact.

- Repeat the activity until everyone has experienced success and has been praised.

- This activity can be extended to help the group continue to practise. Use other scenarios to help people to role play good eye contact. You may choose to video them if you think this may help.

TALKABOUT Body Language ... Facial expression

Topic 3 Facial expression

Activity 13 Watch my face!

Preparation

You may need some large sheets of paper and pens to write down discussion ideas.

Photocopy the worksheet.

You may want to prepare short role plays (modelling) of you and a co-facilitator having a conversation or source a few video clips of people talking to each other. You could use the facial expression clips on the Talkabout DVD as an alternative to the modelling.

Instructions

- Ask the group to watch you and your co-facilitator have a conversation. Use a normal scenario, for example, talking to each other about what you did at the weekend. In the first scenario, one of the group facilitators should use no facial expression while the other person talks normally. Stop and ask the group what they noticed. Was there anything that was not good? Then suggest that you will do better the next time.

- In the second role play, one of you could use excessive and/or inappropriate facial expression (you may want to do this as two separate role plays). Stop and ask the group what they noticed. Was there anything that was not good? You can then talk about facial expression that is too much or inappropriate to the context. Then suggest that you will do better the next time.

- In the third role play, you can use appropriate facial expression.

- At each point, discuss how it makes people appear if they use inappropriate facial expression. Use the phrases from Activity 7 to help.

- The group members can then complete the worksheet.

TALKABOUT Body Language … Facial expression

Activity 13 'Watch my face!' worksheet

Name .... Date ....

Poor facial expression

❶ No facial expression …

> This means our faces don't move much when we are talking or listening in a conversation.
>
> If we don't use any facial expression when we are talking to someone:
>
> The other person may think ....
>
> The other person may feel ....

❷ Inappropriate facial expression …

> This means our faces don't match the words that are being spoken or our faces are too exaggerated in their expression.
>
> If we use inappropriate facial expressions when we are talking to someone:
>
> The other person may think ....
>
> The other person may feel ....

TALKABOUT Body Language ... Facial expression

Activity 14 Why is facial expression important?

Preparation

Use the cards from Activity 9.

Photocopy the worksheet.

Instructions

- Explain to the group that you are going to recap on all of the reasons why eye contact is important and see whether any of them apply to facial expression. So:

    o To help start a conversation – we use more eye contact at the beginning of a conversation but also we need to have a friendly facial expression to encourage someone to want to talk to us.

    o To show people that we are listening – we need to use more eye contact when we are listening than when we are talking and we need to use facial expression that is appropriate to what they are telling us.

    o To show interest – we look at people to let them know we are interested in what they are saying. We widen our eyes to show real interest and use appropriate facial expression.

    o To watch the other person to see how they are feeling – we look at their eyes to see if they are looking at us (good sign!) or looking around the room (not a good sign!). We can also look at their facial expression.

    o To take turns – we use more eye contact as we hand over the conversation to the other person and we use appropriate facial expression to encourage the person to talk to us.

    o To be polite – people like people who make good eye contact and have good facial expression.

- You could demonstrate these points through different role plays (modelling) or you could use the cards to get a discussion going, as in Activity 9.

- The group members can then complete their worksheet.

TALKABOUT Body Language ... Facial expression

Activity 14 'Why is facial expression important?' worksheet

Name .... Date ....

Why is facial expression important?

TALKABOUT Body Language ... Facial expression

Activity 15 Different feelings

Preparation

Collect and print out (or cut out) several faces, from the internet or magazines, showing a few different emotions, for example: happy, sad, angry, bored, scared, embarrassed, worried and excited.

Photocopy some or all of the emotion cards and laminate them if you want to use them again.

You may also need a copy of the worksheet and a large sheet of paper and some glue.

Instructions

- Explain to the group that you are going to consider different facial expressions and what they may look like.

- Go through as many of the cards as is appropriate for the group and discuss the different emotions. Place them on the table.

- Go through the pictures you have collected and agree what the emotion is. These can then either be placed under the corresponding card or stuck on a large piece of paper to create a collage or poster.

Variation

Divide the group into two teams and take it in turns to act out one of the emotions. Can they guess which emotion is being acted?

Take photographs of the group acting out these emotions and stick them on the worksheet.

TALKABOUT Body Language ... Facial expression

Activity 15 'Different feelings' cards

happy

sad

angry

bored

scared

worried

embarrassed

excited

TALKABOUT Body Language ... Facial expression

Activity 15 'Different feelings' worksheet

Name .... Date ....

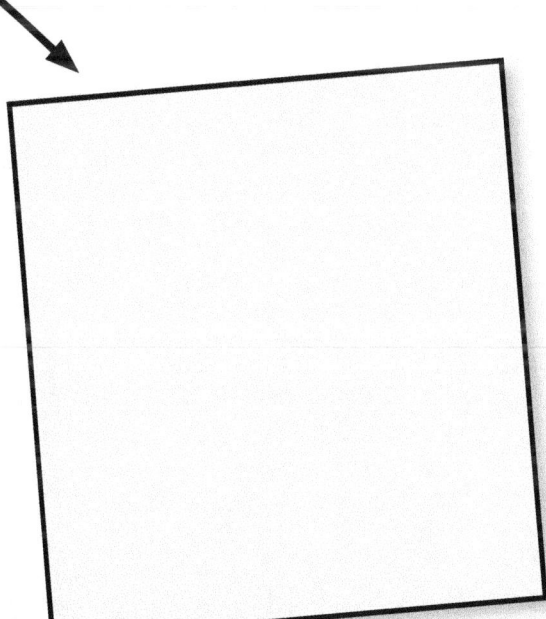

TALKABOUT Body Language ... Facial expression

Activity 16 The rules for facial expression

Preparation

Photocopy the handout. Cut them to size if the group members are going to put these in their A5 fact book.

Instructions

- Explain to the group that you are going to consider the rules for good facial expression.

- Ask the group to consider when it is important to look sad or happy or angry. Think about helping other people to know we are feeling something.

- Then consider the importance of looking sad if someone is saying something sad as this shows people we are listening to them and we are also showing empathy.

- Distribute the handout and discuss what it says.

Note on 'Learning to ...': now consider whether any of the group members need to complete a 'Learning to ...' worksheet on facial expression. If appropriate, refer to Activity 11 'Learning to look' for instructions and the worksheet.

TALKABOUT Body Language ... Facial expression

Activity 16 'The rules for facial expression' handout

Name .... Date ....

Facial expression

What does good facial expression mean?

✓ Good facial expression means that our faces should match what we are saying

✓ If we feel sad then we should look sad – this helps people to know how we feel

✓ We should also make sure that our faces are responding to what the other person is saying

✓ Smiling is a good way to appear more friendly and confident

Why is this important?

We need to use good facial expressions to show people we are listening to them. We can also use our facial expression to show people how we are feeling. Smiling is important to show people that we are friendly and interested. If we use poor facial expressions, people may think we are rude and may not want to talk to us.

TALKABOUT Body Language ... Facial expression

Activity 17 Face your emotions

Preparation

Create some space in the room so that the group members can move around freely.

You will also need a music player and possibly a video recording device.

Instructions

- Explain that you are going to move around the room and when the music stops, or the facilitator says 'Stop', they turn to the person nearest to them. They will then try to use their good facial expression when their partner tells them something.

- You can make this simpler by agreeing a few statements beforehand. Ask the group to come up with some examples, such as:

    o   Tell your partner that your hamster has just died.

    o   Tell your partner that it's your birthday tomorrow.

    o   Tell your partner that you are not feeling very well.

- The group facilitator watches the group and encourages some of the pairs to demonstrate their good facial expression.

- Repeat the activity until everyone has experienced success and has been praised.

- This activity can be extended to help the group continue to practise. Use other scenarios to help people to role play good facial expression. You may choose to video them if you think this may help.

TALKABOUT Body Language ... Gesture

Topic 4 Gesture

Activity 18 Watch my hands!

Preparation

You may need large sheets of paper and pens to write down discussion ideas.

Photocopy the worksheet.

You may want to prepare short role plays (modelling) of you and a co-facilitator having a conversation or source a few video clips of people talking to each other. You could use the gesture clips on the Talkabout DVD as an alternative to the modelling. It is hard to model inappropriate gesture and you will need to practise! Watch the DVD clip for an excellent example.

Instructions

- Ask the group to watch you and your co-facilitator have a conversation. Use a normal scenario, for example, talking to each other about what you did at the weekend. In the first scenario, one facilitator should not use gestures. Make sure that you include things which really needed gestures, eg pointing at or explaining something. The other person could look confused. Stop and ask the group what they noticed. Was there anything that was not good? Then suggest that you will do better the next time.

- In the second role play, one facilitator could use excessive and then inappropriate gesture, for example, making a thumbs-up sign when saying you were not feeling very good (you could do this as two separate role plays). Stop and ask the group what they noticed. Was there anything that was not good? You can then talk about gesture that is too much or inappropriate to the context. Then suggest that you will do better the next time.

- In the third role play, you can use appropriate gesture.

- At each point, talk about how it makes people appear if they use inappropriate gesture. Use the phrases from Activity 7 to help.

- The group members can then complete their worksheet.

TALKABOUT Body Language ... Gesture

Activity 18 'Watch my hands!' worksheet

Name .... Date ....

Poor gesture

❶ No gesture ...

> This means we don't use our hands much when we are talking or listening in a conversation.
>
> If we don't use any gesture when we are talking to someone:
>
> The other person may think ....
>
> The other person may feel ....

❷ Inappropriate gesture ...

> This means our hands move too much when we are talking and are too exaggerated, or it means we use gestures which are inappropriate to the situation.
>
> If we use inappropriate gestures when we are talking to someone:
>
> The other person may think ....
>
> The other person may feel ....

TALKABOUT Body Language ... Gesture

Activity 19 Why is gesture important?

Preparation

Find some television clips of people talking and using gesture. Chat shows are often a good source.

Prepare some scenarios for using no gesture

Photocopy the worksheet.

Instructions

- Explain to the group that they are going to watch a short television clip with the sound off. Group members will watch and note down every time someone uses their hands. Ask the group why they thought they were using the gesture. Watch the clip again and see if they were right.

- Then ask the group members to prepare a short role play or conversation where they are going to try to talk about something while sitting on their hands. Good suggestions for this are giving directions to someone, telling someone how big or tall something or someone is, and describing how to play an instrument or play a sport.

- The group talk about how it felt to use no gesture and what it looked like to watch other people using no gesture.

- The group members can then complete their worksheet.

TALKABOUT Body Language ... Gesture

Activity 19 'Why is gesture important?' worksheet

Name .... Date ....

Why is gesture important?

TALKABOUT Body Language ... Gesture

Activity 20 Different gestures

Preparation

Collect and print or cut out pictures of gestures, for example: pointed finger (angry or irritated), arms folded (bored), hands over mouth (scared), clenched fists (angry), open palms (happy or relaxed), head in hands (worried or stressed), hand clap (excited), and hands on cheeks (embarrassed).

Photocopy the worksheet.

You can also use the emotion cards from Activity 15 'Different feelings'.

Instructions

- Explain to the group that they are going to consider different gestures and what those may be telling us.

- Go through the pictures and ask the group to think about how the person may be feeling. Choose the emotion card that best fits the picture.

- Then consider what they may be saying, for example 'Don't do that!' or 'I'm not interested'. If you feel these ideas will be difficult to generate, think of some examples and ask the group to sort them accordingly. For example:

Pointed finger	ANGRY	'Don't do that!'
Arms folded	BORED	'I'm not interested'
Hand over mouth	SCARED	'Oh no, that's horrible!'
Clenched fists	ANGRY	'I can't believe she just said that!'
Open palms	HAPPY	'What do you think?'
Head in hands	WORRIED	'I've got too much to do!'
Hands on cheeks	EMBARRASSED	'Oh no, I'm so silly'

- The group members can then complete their worksheet.

TALKABOUT Body Language ... Gesture

Activity 20 'Different gestures' worksheet

Name .... Date ....

Gestures   What are they saying?   How are they feeling?

TALKABOUT Body Language ... Gesture

Activity 21 The rules for gesture

Preparation

Photocopy the handout. Cut them to size if the group members are going to put them in their A5 fact book.

Instructions

- Explain to the group that they are going to consider the rules for good gesture.

- Ask the group to consider when is it important to use gesture?

- Then consider the importance of using gesture to back up what we are saying and helping people to understand what we are saying.

- Distribute the handout and discuss what it says.

Note on 'Learning to …': now consider whether any of the group members need to complete a 'Learning to …' worksheet on gesture. If appropriate, refer to Activity 11 'Learning to look' for instructions and the worksheet.

TALKABOUT Body Language ... Gesture

Activity 21 'The rules for gesture' handout

Name .... Date ....

Gesture

What does good gesture mean?

✓ Using gesture helps people to listen to us and understand what we are saying

✓ It should back up what we are saying and not be a distraction

✓ Using gesture can make us look more confident and interesting to listen to

✓ Try to remember to use open hands to appear more friendly

! Why is this important?

We need to use gestures to help reinforce what we are saying. Remember that our gestures will also tell people how we are feeling: for example, when we are nervous, our hands may move more and we may touch our face. If we don't use gestures at all, or we use inappropriate gestures, it can be distracting for the other person. We may look tense or nervous.

TALKABOUT Body Language ... Gesture

Activity 22 Give us a hand

Preparation

Photocopy and cut out the prompt cards and laminate them if you want to use them again.

You will also need the different feelings cards from Activity 15.

Create a space in the room for people to move around and act out their scenario.

You may also like to have a video recording device ready to record group members' good use of gesture.

Instructions

- Explain to the group that you are going to act out something using no words, just lots of gesture and body language.

- Start with the emotion cards. Take it in turns to take a card and act it out. Can everyone guess what emotion they are trying to act out?

- Repeat the activity with the scenario cards and see if they can guess what the card says. They may like to choose their own scenarios rather than use the ones provided here.

- Continue the activity until everyone has had a turn.

- This activity can be extended to help the group continue to practise. Use other scenarios to help people to role play good gesture. You may choose to video them if you think this may help.

TALKABOUT Body Language ... Gesture

Activity 22 'Give us a hand' cards

| I have lost my cat – have you seen it? |

| I have won the lottery! |

| I went fishing and caught a big fish. |

| I have eaten too much and now I feel ill. |

| Be quiet! It's too noisy in here. |

| I watched a film that was very scary. |

| I was playing football and scored a goal. |

| I had to run to catch the bus. |

| I went for a walk and got wet in the rain. |

TALKABOUT Body Language ... Distance

Topic 5 Distance

Activity 23 Watch the distance!

Preparation

You will need a large sheet of paper and pens to write down discussion ideas.

Photocopy the worksheet.

You may want to prepare short role plays (modelling) of you and a co-facilitator having a conversation or source a few video clips of people talking to each other. You could use the distance clips on the Talkabout DVD as an alternative to the modelling. Inappropriate distance can be shown in two ways and must not be confused with touch when modelling being too close or volume when modelling being too far apart.

Instructions

- Ask the group to watch you and your co-facilitator have a conversation. Use a normal scenario, for example, talking to each other about what you did at the weekend. In the first scenario, one of the group facilitators should walk up and stand right in front of the other (it is best to stand side-on to the group to show this). The second facilitator should look uncomfortable and may even take a step back. The first facilitator should step forward again, to close the distance, but be careful not to touch them. Stop and ask the group what they noticed. Was there anything that was not good? Then suggest that you will do better the next time.

- In the second role play, begin on opposite sides of the room. The same facilitator as above starts the conversation but remains where they are. Have the conversation in this way but be careful not to shout. Stop and ask the group what they noticed. Was there anything that was not good? The facilitators could then walk towards each other and ask the group to tell them where they should stop. Then suggest that one arm's length is a good rule and that you will do better the next time.

- In the third role play, you can use appropriate distance.

- At each point, talk about how it makes people appear if they use inappropriate distance and how it makes others feel. Use the phrases from Activity 7 to help.

- The group members can then complete their worksheet.

TALKABOUT Body Language ... Distance

Activity 23 'Watch the distance!' worksheet

Name .... Date ....

Poor distance

1 Too close ...

> This means we stand too close to people when we are talking or listening to them in a conversation or get in their personal space.
>
> If we stand too close when we are talking to someone:
>
> The other person may think ....
>
> The other person may feel ....

2 Too far away ...

> This means we stand too far away from someone when we are talking to them in a conversation.
>
> If we stand too far away from someone when we are talking to them:
>
> The other person may think ....
>
> The other person may feel ....

TALKABOUT Body Language ... Distance

Activity 24 That's a close one!

Preparation

You will need a very large sheet of paper (eg four pieces of flipchart paper stuck together). Draw a pair of feet in the middle of one of the short edges and then two semi-circles, one within one arm's length of the feet and one just a bit further away.

You may also want to use a camera and a tape measure (optional).

Instructions

- Explain to the group that you are going to be considering how close you can get to different people.

- Ask one group member to come and stand on the feet on the large sheet of paper.

- Then ask another group member to come up and stand face-to-face with the group member who is on the paper feet so that they both feel comfortable. When they have agreed, draw around the second group member's feet and write in their names, eg 'Ollie and Murphy'. You may like to take a photograph too.

- You can also ask them to hold out their arms and see if they are one arm's length away – the standard rule for distance.

- Then ask another group member to come up and test out their distance with the first group member and add their feet to the paper.

- Continue until every group member has had a turn standing on the feet and in the circles on the paper.

- Are there any differences in the group? Was anyone closer than one arm's length away? Are they close friends?

- Who would they allow to get closer and stand in their inner circle? (eg mum, best friend, grandparent)

Variation

Use a tape measure to measure the distances between each pair. Create a table of these measurements and compare the differences.

TALKABOUT Body Language … Distance

Activity 25 Closer to you?

Preparation

Photocopy the worksheet. You may like to enlarge this to A3 size if you are discussing it as a group or make several A4 copies if working individually or in pairs.

You may also need the large sheet of paper from Activity 24.

Instructions

- Remind the group of the activity completed in the previous session, looking at how close the group members could get to each other. You may like to get out the large sheet from the previous activity.

- Explain to the group that today you are going to be thinking about when the one arm's length rule might change.

- Put the worksheet in the middle of the group and start by getting them to think about the people who we don't mind getting closer than one arm's length to us, eg Mum and Dad, siblings, family, best friend, people we like and know well.

- If a group member suggests someone different (for example, their social worker), ask them why and challenge this if it is not appropriate.

- Next, ask the group to think of a situation where the rules may change and people who are not on the first list may get closer to us, eg in a lift, at a party, at a funeral or wedding, in a queue, at the doctor's or dentist's surgery. Talk about each one, how it may change and why this is OK in this situation.

- The group can then fill in their worksheet.

Variations

The group could complete the worksheet in pairs and then share their ideas with the rest of the group.

The group facilitators could prepare several situation cards. The group members then take it in turns to choose one and discuss how distance may be affected or change in that scenario.

TALKABOUT Body Language ... Distance

Activity 25 'Closer to you?' worksheet

Name .... Date ....

Who?
Can you think of a few people who you can get close to? Make a list of their names here:

....
....
....
....
....
....
....

When?
Sometimes you have to get close to people who are not on your list. When might this happen?

....
....
....
....
....
....
....

TALKABOUT Body Language ... Distance

Activity 26 The rules for distance

Preparation

Photocopy the handout. Cut them to size if the group members are going to put them in their A5 fact book.

You may also need the worksheet from Activity 11.

Instructions

- Explain to the group that you are going to consider the rules for good distance.

- Ask the group to consider what we mean by good distance and when this may alter.

- Then consider the importance of getting distance right in a conversation to make people feel comfortable talking to us and how they might react if this is wrong.

- Distribute the handout and discuss what it says.

Note on 'Learning to ...': now consider whether any of the group members need to complete a 'Learning to ...' worksheet on distance. If appropriate, refer to Activity 11 'Learning to look' for instructions and the worksheet.

TALKABOUT Body Language ... Distance

Activity 26 'The rules for distance' handout

Name .... Date ....

Distance

What does good distance mean?

✓ We don't usually like people to stand closer than one arm's length to us

✓ If we know the person really well and like them then they may be able to get closer

✓ If we are in a small space, like a lift, we can get closer to someone but it's best to stand sideways

✓ If people are taller than us, or we don't know them well, then we like them to stand a bit further away

Why is this important?

! We need to get our distance right to be polite. We can use our good distance to show someone that we are listening and that we like them or care about them. If we get our distance wrong and stand too close, people may not want to talk to us as they may feel uncomfortable or intimidated.

TALKABOUT Body Language … Distance

Activity 27 Mind the gap!

Preparation

Create a space in the room for people to move about and act out their scenarios.

Instructions

- Explain to the group that you are going to act out different scenarios and practise using your good distance rules.

- The group should work in pairs and use the scenarios that they came up with in Activity 25. Give each pair a scenario and then give them time to create a little role play around it.

- Each pair must decide who they are in the situation and then plan the appropriate distance they will need to achieve.

- Each pair takes it in turns to perform these role plays to the group. You could keep the scenario secret, so that the group members have to guess it, and then comment on whether the distance was appropriate for it.

TALKABOUT Body Language ... Touch

Topic 6 Touch

Activity 28 Watch my touch!

Preparation

You may need large sheets of paper and pens to write down group discussion ideas.

Photocopy the worksheet.

You may want to prepare short role plays (modelling) of you and a co-facilitator having a conversation or source a few video clips of people talking to each other. You could use the touch clips on the Talkabout DVD as an alternative to the modelling. Inappropriate touch can be shown in two ways and must not be confused with distance or gestures when modelling.

Instructions

- Ask the group to watch you and your co-facilitator have a conversation. In the first scenario, try to show inappropriate 'no touch'. You could use a scenario where one person is upset: for example, their pet is ill. The other facilitator should look and sound sympathetic but not use any touch, even when the first person asks for a hug or indicates that they need comfort, eg 'I could do with a hug'. Stop and ask the group what they noticed. Was there anything that was not good? Then suggest that you will do better the next time. **Note:** if 'no touch' is too subtle for the group, go straight on to the second role play.

- In the second role play, begin the same conversation but, this time, the second facilitator responds by overreacting, giving the other person constant hugs, rubbing their head or hair too much, holding or rubbing their hand or leg. The first facilitator should look uncomfortable and attempt to pull away from the touches, to show they are inappropriate. Ask the group what they thought and discuss whether anything was wrong. Then suggest that we do need to use touch to comfort someone, or to greet or show interest, but it has to be appropriate to the context and setting. Suggest that you will do better the next time.

- In the third role play, you can use appropriate touch.

- At each point, talk about how it makes people appear if they use inappropriate touch and how it makes others feel. Use the phrases from Activity 7 to help.

- The group members can then complete their worksheet.

TALKABOUT Body Language ... Touch

Activity 28 'Watch my touch!' worksheet

Name .... Date ....

Poor touch

❶ No touch ...

This means we don't touch someone when talking to them, even if it is appropriate, for example, if they are upset or worried.

If we use no touch when we are talking to someone:

The other person may think ....

The other person may feel ....

❷ Inappropriate touch ...

This means we touch someone when talking to them but it is the wrong kind of touch or not right for the situation.

If we touch someone inappropriately when we are talking to them:

The other person may think ....

The other person may feel ....

TALKABOUT Body Language ... Touch

Activity 29 Touch control

Preparation

You will need to photocopy the two sets of cards. They can be cut out and laminated if you want to use them again.

Photocopy the worksheet.

Instructions

- Explain to the group that you are going to be considering different types of touch and who they could use these with.

- Place the two sets of cards in separate piles and face-down in the middle of the group.

- Ask the first group member to select one card from each pile – one touch card and one scenario card.

- The group member then considers whether this is an appropriate touch to use in that situation or not. The group can help decide this if they are struggling.

- Continue the activity until all of the cards have been selected.

- Next, match up cards and scenarios – what is the appropriate touch in each situation? You can use the touch cards more than once.

- Discuss any differences in the group and challenge any that you feel may be inappropriate.

- The group members can then complete an individual worksheet with the types of touch they would use in each scenario.

TALKABOUT Body Language ... Touch

Activity 29 'Touch control' cards

shake hands

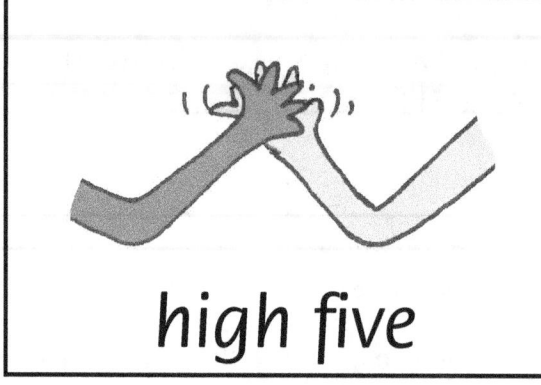
high five

pat on back

hold hands

hug

kiss

touch elbow

no touch

TALKABOUT Body Language … Touch

Activity 29 'Touch control' scenario cards

Saying 'Hello' at an interview.	Greeting your friend when you see them in town.
Walking to the shops with your five-year-old niece.	Saying 'Hello' to your grandma.
Saying 'Hello' to your doctor.	Talking to a shopkeeper.
Meeting someone for the first time.	Comforting a friend.

TALKABOUT Body Language ... Touch

Activity 29 'Touch control' worksheet

Name .... Date ....

Write in the appropriate touch you could use in each of the scenarios below. You could use some more than once.

☆ Saying 'Hello' at an interview ⟶ ☐

☆ Greeting your friend when you see them in town ⟶ ☐

☆ Walking to the shops with your five-year-old niece ⟶ ☐

☆ Saying 'Hello' to your grandma ⟶ ☐

☆ Saying 'Hello' to your doctor ⟶ ☐

☆ Talking to a shopkeeper ⟶ ☐

☆ Meeting someone for the first time ⟶ ☐

☆ Comforting a friend ⟶ ☐

TALKABOUT Body Language ... Touch

Activity 30 Why is touch important?

Preparation

Find some video clips from a television programme of people talking and using touch.

Photocopy the worksheet.

Have paper and pens out for the group members to write down ideas.

Instructions

- Explain to the group that you are going to watch a short clip of a television programme. The group members should watch it and write down every time that someone uses touch.

- Ask the group why they thought the people were using the touch. Watch the video clip again and see if they were right.

- The group then discuss why they think touch is important when talking to someone. The reasons may include:

    o to greet someone

    o to show we care

    o to comfort someone

    o to show we are interested

    o to show we are listening

    o to end a conversation.

- The group members can then complete their worksheet.

TALKABOUT Body Language ... Touch

Activity 30 'Why is touch important?' worksheet

Name .... Date ....

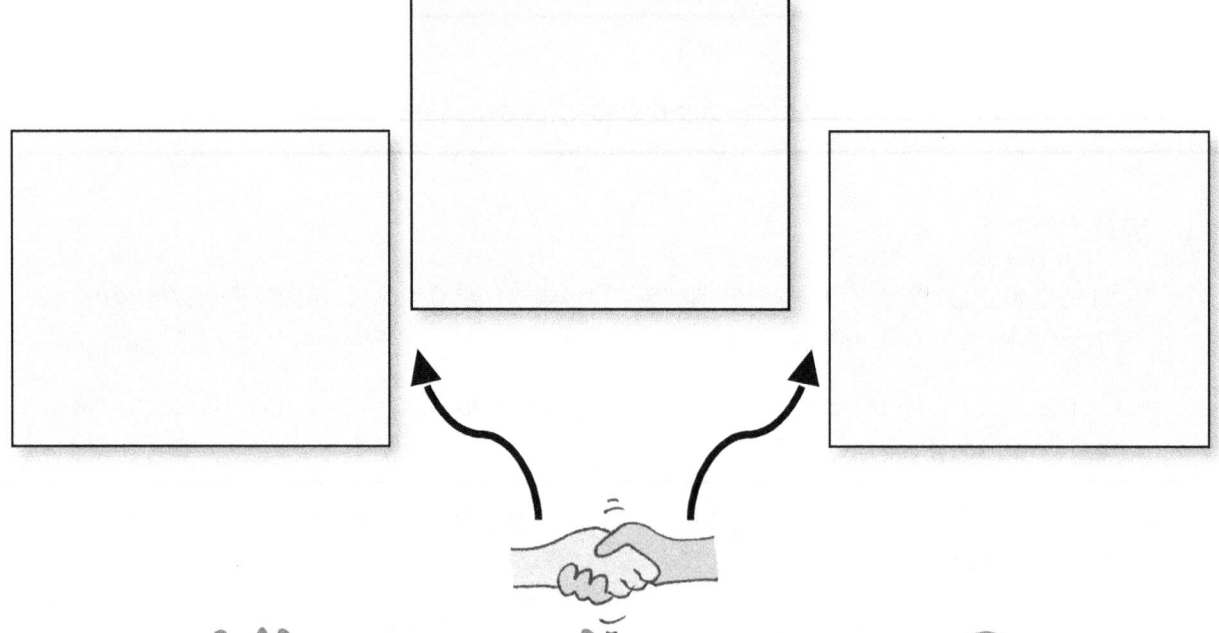

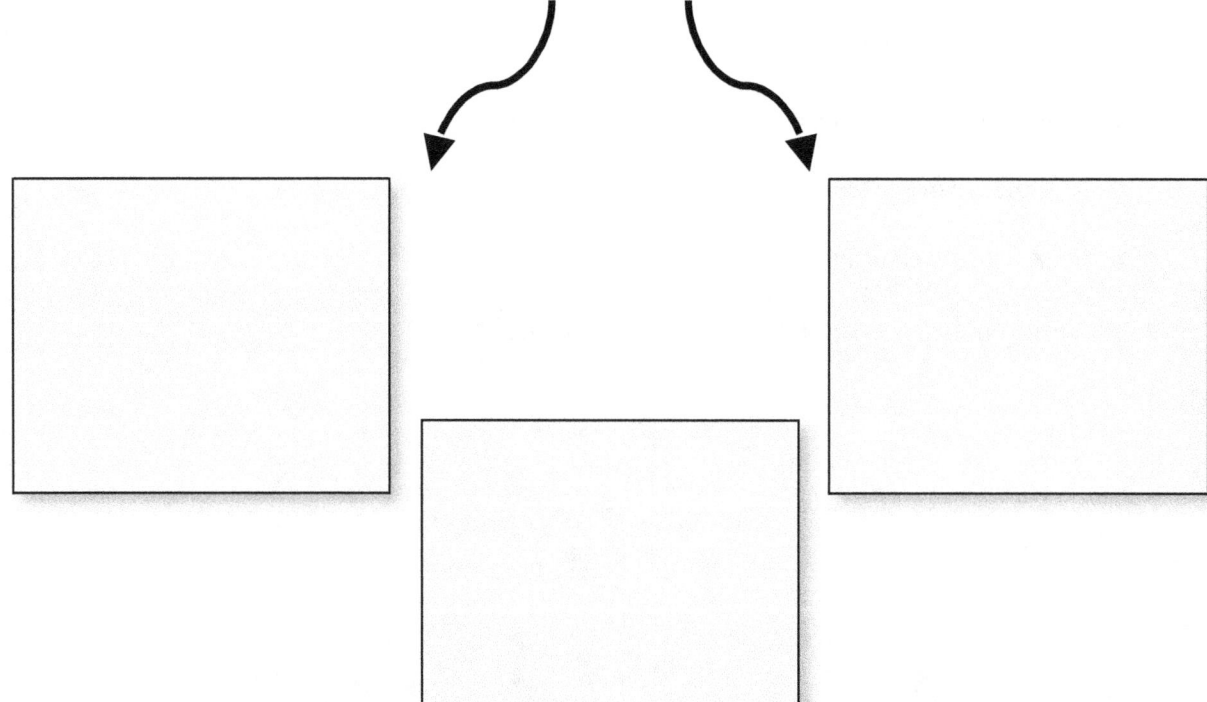

Why is touch important?

TALKABOUT Body Language ... Touch

Activity 31 The rules for touch

Preparation

Photocopy the handout. Cut them to size if the group members are going to put them in their A5 fact book.

You may also need the worksheet from Activity 11.

Instructions

- Explain to the group that you are going to consider the rules for good touch.

- Ask the group to consider what we mean by 'good touch' and when this may alter.

- Then consider the importance of getting touch right in a conversation, to make people feel comfortable talking to us, and how they might react if this is wrong.

- Distribute the handout and discuss what it says.

Note on 'Learning to ...': now consider whether any of the group members need to complete a 'Learning to ...' worksheet on touch. If appropriate, refer to Activity 11 'Learning to look' for instructions and the worksheet.

Activity 31 'The rules for touch' handout

Name .... Date ....

Touch

What does good touch mean?

 ✓ Touch can be an important part of having a conversation. If we know the person really well, we may greet them by giving them a high five or a hug

 ✓ If they are upset, we may put our arm around them or hug them

 ✓ If we don't know people well, we could shake hands with them or wave

 ✓ Touch may change depending on the situation and the age of the person we are talking to

! Why is this important?

It is important to get our touch right when talking to someone so that we don't make them feel uncomfortable. We can use touch to say 'Hello', comfort someone and show that we care about them. If we use the wrong touch with someone, they may feel embarrassed or unsafe and not want to talk to us any more.

TALKABOUT Body Language ... Touch

Activity 32 To touch or not to touch?

Preparation

Photocopy and cut out the scenario cards and laminate them if you want to use them again.

Clear enough space in the room for the group members to move around and role play appropriate touch.

Instructions

- Explain to the group that you are going to act out different scenarios and practise using your good touch rules.

- The group should work in pairs and each pair should be given one scenario. Give them time to create a little role play around that situation. They may like to add to the scenario, to make it as relevant to their experience as possible. Or the group may choose their own scenarios if the ones given are not appropriate.

- Each pair decides who they are in the scenario and they then plan the role play using appropriate touch.

- **Note:** make sure that everyone is comfortable taking part in this activity, particularly with any use of touch.

- The pairs then take it in turns to perform their role play to the group. The group could discuss whether everyone agrees with their choice of touch. Would anyone have done something different? Consider the important factor that some people use and like touch more than others and we must always take this into account

TALKABOUT Body Language ... Touch

Activity 32 'To touch or not to touch' scenarios

| Your friend has just given you a brilliant gift |

| You meet up with your friend in town |

| You are upset because your phone has been stolen |

| You are meeting your favourite aunt who lives in Australia – you haven't seen her for a year |

| You are walking into an interview and introducing yourself to the person who is interviewing you |

| You are chatting to your local shopkeeper |

| Your friend is excited – she has just told you she is getting married |

TALKABOUT Body Language ... Fidgeting

Topic 7 Fidgeting

Activity 33 Watch me fidget!

Preparation

You will need large sheets of paper and pens to write down group discussion ideas.

Photocopy the worksheet.

You may want to prepare short role plays (modelling) of you and a co-facilitator having a conversation or source a few video clips of people talking to each other. You could use the fidgeting clips on the Talkabout DVD as an alternative to the modelling.

Instructions

- Ask the group to watch you and your co-facilitator have a conversation. Use a normal scenario: for example, talking to each other about what you did at the weekend. In the first scenario, one group facilitator should fidget excessively while the second tries to continue the conversation. Stop and ask the group what they noticed. Was there anything that was not good?

- In the second role play, the first group facilitator should sit very rigidly on their hands and not move at all. Make it very obvious that this is inappropriate. Stop and ask the group what they noticed. Suggest that the first facilitator was better and didn't fidget but was there anything that was not good? Then suggest that you will do better the next time.

- In the third role play, you can use appropriate fidgeting or movement.

- At each point, talk about how it makes people appear if they use inappropriate fidgeting and how it makes others feel. Use the phrases from Activity 7 to help.

- The group members can then complete their worksheet.

TALKABOUT Body Language ... Fidgeting

Activity 33 'Watch me fidget!' worksheet

Name .... Date ....

Fidgeting

❶ Too much fidgeting ...

> This means we fidget a lot when we are talking to someone. We may move our legs and hands, or fiddle with objects or with our clothing.
>
> If we fidget too much when we are talking to someone:
>
> The other person may think ....
>
> The other person may feel ....

❷ No movement at all ...

> This means we sit very rigidly, with no movement, when we are talking to someone.
>
> If we don't use any movements at all:
>
> The other person may think ....
>
> The other person may feel ....

TALKABOUT Body Language ... Fidgeting

Activity 34 Why do people fidget?

Preparation

You will need a large piece of paper or a wipe board and pens for recording the discussion. Alternatively, you could enlarge the worksheet to A3 size for the group discussion.

Photocopy the worksheet.

Instructions

- Ask the group to think about all of the different types of fidgeting, for example:
    - fiddling with objects
    - fiddling with hair
    - touching earrings or other jewellery
    - touching face
    - wringing hands
    - wiggling legs
    - tapping on the table
    - moving whole body.
- Ask the group to think about why people fidget, for example:
    - they are nervous
    - they feel cold
    - they are bored
    - they feel excited
    - they need to go to the toilet
    - they have sensory difficulties
    - it helps them to concentrate.
- The group members can then complete their worksheet (optional).

Activity 34 'Why do people fidget?' worksheet

Name .... Date ....

Different ways we fidget

❓ **Can you think of 5 reasons why people fidget?**

1. ....
2. ....
3. ....
4. ....
5. ....

TALKABOUT Body Language ... Fidgeting

Activity 35 The rules for fidgeting

Preparation

Photocopy the handout. Cut them to size if the group members are going to put them in their A5 fact book.

You may also need the worksheet for Activity 11.

Instructions

- Explain to the group that you are going to consider the rules for fidgeting.

- Ask the group to consider what we mean by 'not fidgeting' and when it may be harder to do this.

- Then consider the importance of getting it right in a conversation, so that people feel comfortable talking to us, and how they might react if this is wrong.

- Distribute the handout and discuss what it says.

Note on 'Learning to ...': now consider whether any of the group members need to complete a 'Learning to ...' worksheet on not fidgeting. If appropriate, refer to Activity 11 'Learning to look' for instructions and the worksheet.

Activity 35 'The rules for fidgeting' handout

Name .... Date ....

Fidgeting

What does good touch mean?

✓ It is natural to move a bit when we are talking to someone

✓ We may move our hands or bodies to express something, such as excitement or shock, or to describe something

✓ Fidgeting is when our movements become distracting to the other person

✓ Fidgeting is when we fiddle with things or our bodies or clothing

Why is this important?

If we fidget when we are talking to people, it will look as if we are not listening or we are bored. People may not want to talk to us because it is distracting to talk to someone who is fidgeting a lot. It may also make them feel uncomfortable or angry.

TALKABOUT Body Language ... Posture

Topic 8 Posture

Activity 36 Watch my posture!

Preparation

You may need large sheets of paper and pens to write down the group discussion ideas.

Photocopy the worksheet.

You may want to prepare short role plays (modelling) of you and a co-facilitator having a conversation or source a few video clips of people talking to each other. You could use the posture clips on the Talkabout DVD as an alternative to the modelling. Inappropriate posture can be shown in two ways: too relaxed or slouching and too tense.

Instructions

- Ask the group to watch you and your co-facilitator have a conversation. Use a normal scenario, for example, what you are doing next weekend. In the first scenario, one group facilitator's posture should be overly relaxed, eg slouched over the desk or back on their chair, legs and arms stretched out. Remember to keep facial expression and eye contact as appropriate as possible. Stop and ask the group what they noticed. Was there anything that was not good?

- In the second role play, begin the same conversation but, this time, the group facilitator's posture should be overly tense, for example, sitting upright and very rigid. They should retain this posture throughout. Ask the group what they thought and discuss whether anything was wrong. Then suggest that posture tells us a lot about how someone is feeling and that we adapt it to be appropriate to the context and setting. Suggest that you will do better the next time.

- In the third role play, you can use appropriate posture.

- At each point, talk about how it makes people appear if they use inappropriate posture and how it makes others feel. Use the phrases from Activity 7 to help.

- The group members can then complete their worksheet.

TALKABOUT Body Language ... Posture

Activity 36 'Watch my posture!' worksheet

Name .... Date ....

Poor posture

① Too relaxed ...

This means we slouch over furniture and may stretch our legs and arms out or we may be hunched over.

If our posture is too relaxed when we are talking to someone:

The other person may think ....

The other person may feel ....

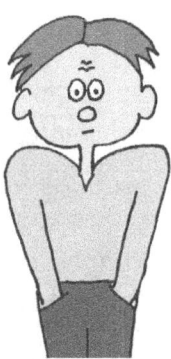

② Too tense ...

This means we sit or stand up very straight, head up, with arms and legs rigid and tense.

If our posture is too tense when we are talking to someone:

The other person may think ....

The other person may feel ....

TALKABOUT Body Language ... Posture

Activity 37 Walk this way

Preparation

Clear enough space in the room to allow the group members to walk around freely.

You could also have a camera to take photographs of the group completing the activity.

Instructions

- Explain to the group that they are going to stand up and think about their bodies. Then give them the following instructions.

- Make yourselves as **tall** as possible – raise your head, straighten your back, etc. Stop and look around the room. How do we all look?

- Make yourselves as **small** as possible – huddle into a ball, bring your head down, etc. Stop and look around the room. How do we all look?

- Imagine you are really **angry** – make your body and face look angry and then walk across the room. Stop and look around the room. How do we all look?

- Imagine you are really **sleepy** – make your body and face look sleepy and walk across the room. Find a chair and sit down sleepily. Stop and look around the room. How do we all look?

- Ask the group to think about how they changed their posture according to the instructions and how they were feeling. Introduce the terms **tense** and **relaxed**.

TALKABOUT Body Language ... Posture

Activity 38 Posture thermometer

Preparation

Photocopy the thermometer – it is best enlarged to A3 size.

You will also need the emotions cards from Activity 15 'Different feelings'.

Instructions

- Start by reintroducing the terms 'tense' and 'relaxed'.

- Then show the group the thermometer and explain that sometimes our bodies are really tense, sometimes they are really relaxed and sometimes they are in the middle.

- Help the group members to feel familiar with the thermometer and rating scale by asking them to sit in a number 5 posture (really tense), a number 1 posture (really relaxed) and then number 3 (normal posture).

- Next, using the feelings cards, select the first card and read out the emotion. Ask the group to imagine feeling like that and then sit in a way to show it, eg if 'sad' is selected, sit in a sad way, hunched over, head down.

- Then ask the group to look around at everyone's posture and rate it on the thermometer. You can place the emotion card next to the rating on the thermometer.

- Work through until all of the emotions have been rated.

TALKABOUT Body Language ... Posture

Activity 38 'Posture thermometer' worksheet

TALKABOUT Body Language ... Posture

Activity 39 Different postures

Preparation

You will need to collect several images from the internet or magazines of different postures. Make sure that they are large enough for all of the group to see.

You will also need the posture thermometer from the previous activity.

Instructions

- Explain to the group that you are going to look at other people's postures today.

- Place the first image in the middle of the group and talk about what they see. Where would they rate it on the posture thermometer?

- Next, ask the group what their initial impression of this person is. What do they think of them? Words they may use include nervous, friendly, arrogant, open, closed, tense and confident.

- Explain to the group that posture is very important when we meet people for the first time because it is one of the main areas of our body language that people judge us on. We will need to think about this especially if we are going to a job interview or meeting someone for the first time.

- Choose another image and repeat the process. Continue until you have discussed several different postures and the initial impressions they give.

TALKABOUT Body Language ... Posture

Activity 40 The rules for posture

Preparation

Photocopy the handout. Cut them to size if the group members are going to put them in their A5 fact book.

You may also need the worksheet from Activity 11.

Instructions

- Explain to the group that you are going to consider the rules for good posture.

- Ask the group to consider what we mean by 'good posture' and when this may alter.

- Then consider the importance of getting posture right in a conversation, to make people feel comfortable talking to us, and how they might react if this is wrong.

- Also consider what initial impressions we give with our posture and how we should adapt it when meeting new people or in a formal setting, for example.

- Distribute the handout and discuss what it says.

Note on 'Learning to ...': now consider whether any of the group members need to complete a 'Learning to ...' worksheet on posture. If appropriate, refer to Activity 11 'Learning to look' for instructions and the worksheet.

Activity 40 'The rules for posture' handout

Name .... Date ....

Posture

What does good posture mean?

✓ Posture is important when talking to someone

✓ When we meet someone, we decide whether we like them within 7 seconds and this is partly based on their posture

✓ Sometimes we should sit upright to show respect, for example in a formal setting

✓ Our posture can also show the other person that we are listening to them

✓ Posture will change depending on the situation and the person we are talking to. For example, sometimes it is OK to be more relaxed

Why is this important?

It is important to get our posture right when meeting and talking to someone, so that they don't think we are being rude. We can use our posture to show respect, to show we are listening and also to show how we are feeling. If we use the wrong posture with someone, they may feel like we are being rude, are not interested or don't want to talk to them.

TALKABOUT Body Language ... Posture

Activity 41 Time to pose!

Preparation

Clear enough space in the room to allow the group members to act out their scenarios.

Instructions

- Explain to the group that you are going to act out different scenarios and practise using good posture.

- Good scenarios are: a job interview, meeting a friend for coffee, complaining at a hotel, giving a talk in a meeting, meeting someone new at the bus stop and going to the cinema with a friend.

- The group should work in pairs. Give each pair a scenario and time to create a little role play around that situation. The pair must decide who they are in the scenario and then plan the appropriate posture they will use.

- The pairs then take it in turns to perform their role play to the group.

TALKABOUT Body Language ... Personal appearance

Topic 9 Personal appearance

Activity 42 Watch my appearance!

Preparation

You may need some large sheets of paper and pens to write down group discussion ideas.

Photocopy the worksheet.

You may want to prepare short role plays (modelling) of you and a co-facilitator having a conversation or source a few video clips of people talking to each other. You could use the personal appearance clips on the Talkabout DVD as an alternative to the modelling.

Instructions

- Ask the group to watch you and your co-facilitator have a conversation. Use a normal scenario, for example, talking to each other about what you did at the weekend. In the first scenario, one group facilitator should enter the room looking scruffy and untidy, eg shirt untucked, a stain or mark on their top, food around their mouth, hair not brushed or untidy. The second facilitator should respond to the conversation as normal but also appear distracted by their appearance: for example, looking them up and down. Stop and ask the group what they noticed. Was there anything that was not good?

- In the second role play, the first group facilitator should enter the room inappropriately dressed, eg wearing a woolly scarf, hat and gloves and a big coat or dressed too smartly. The two facilitators then talk about their day together at the beach and what they will do when they get there. The second facilitator should look at the first as above and may even ask questions such as 'Are you sure that's what you want to wear to the beach?' Stop and ask the group what they noticed. Suggest that the first facilitator looked better and was dressed clean and tidy but was there anything that was not good? Then suggest that you will do better the next time.

- In the third role play, both facilitators are dressed appropriately and discuss their day out to the beach.

- At each point, talk about how it makes people appear if they dress inappropriately and how it makes others feel. Use the phrases from Activity 7 to help.

- The group members can then complete their worksheet.

TALKABOUT Body Language ... Personal appearance

Activity 42 'Watch my appearance!' worksheet

Name .... Date ....

Personal appearance

❶ Untidy/unclean ...

This means we forget to wash or brush our teeth, we may not brush our hair or have it cut and our clothes may be dirty or untidy.

If we are untidy or unclean:

The other person may think ....

The other person may feel ....

❷ Inappropriate dress ...

This means we wear clothes that are not suited to the occasion, the setting or the season. We may wear a scarf in hot weather or a suit to go bowling with friends.

If we don't dress appropriately:

The other person may think ....

The other person may feel ....

TALKABOUT Body Language ... Personal appearance

Activity 43 Looking good!

Preparation

Photocopy the worksheet. It is best enlarged to A3 size if you are working in a group.

Instructions

- Explain to the group that today you are going to be thinking about personal appearance and what we mean by 'appropriate appearance'.

- Ask the group to think about what we mean by appropriate appearance. Encourage them to think about appropriate clothes depending on the setting, situation, season, appropriate accessories, cleanliness, smell, hair, facial hair, etc. Talk about how all of these factors are involved in appropriate appearance.

- Then ask the group why they think appearance is important. Why do we need to worry? You can talk about confidence, belonging, identity, and social rules such as at funerals.

- The group then think about when it is OK to be different and express ourselves, eg at a party, at home, seeing friends, and when it is not OK to express ourselves, eg in some jobs, at formal occasions or at school.

- The group can then fill in their worksheet.

Variation

This activity could be done in two groups or in pairs and then the ideas can be shared and compared.

TALKABOUT Body Language ... Personal appearance

Activity 43 'Looking good!' worksheet

What does appropriate appearance mean?

✓ **When is it OK to express ourselves?**

✗ **When is it not OK to express ourselves?**

Activity 44 The rules for personal appearance

Preparation

Photocopy the handout. Cut them to size if the group members are going to put them in their A5 fact book.

You may also need the worksheet from Activity 11.

Instructions

- Explain to the group that you are going to consider the rules around personal appearance.

- Ask the group to consider what we mean by this and when personal appearance can change.

- Then consider the importance of getting it right when meeting and talking to people, so that they feel comfortable and don't get the wrong impression about us.

- Distribute the handout and discuss what it says.

Note on 'Learning to …': now consider whether any of the group members need to complete a 'Learning to …' worksheet on personal appearance. If appropriate, refer to Activity 11 'Learning to look' for instructions and the worksheet.

TALKABOUT Body Language ... Personal appearance

Activity 43 'Looking good!' worksheet

What does appropriate appearance mean?

✓ **When is it OK to express ourselves?**

✗ **When is it not OK to express ourselves?**

TALKABOUT Body Language ... Personal appearance

Activity 44 The rules for personal appearance

Preparation

Photocopy the handout. Cut them to size if the group members are going to put them in their A5 fact book.

You may also need the worksheet from Activity 11.

Instructions

- Explain to the group that you are going to consider the rules around personal appearance.

- Ask the group to consider what we mean by this and when personal appearance can change.

- Then consider the importance of getting it right when meeting and talking to people, so that they feel comfortable and don't get the wrong impression about us.

- Distribute the handout and discuss what it says.

Note on 'Learning to ...': now consider whether any of the group members need to complete a 'Learning to ...' worksheet on personal appearance. If appropriate, refer to Activity 11 'Learning to look' for instructions and the worksheet.

TALKABOUT Body Language ... Personal appearance

Activity 44 'The rules for personal appearance' handout

Name .... Date ....

Personal appearance
What does good posture mean?

- ✓ Our personal appearance is important when talking to people

- ✓ When we meet someone, we decide whether we like them within 7 seconds and this is partly based on how someone is dressed, looks and smells

- ✓ We need to wear the right clothes appropriate to a situation, setting or season

- ✓ We need to make sure we are clean and our hair is appropriate too

Why is this important?

If we wear the wrong clothes or our appearance is inappropriate, people may think we don't care, that we are lazy or rude, and they may get the wrong impression of us. People may feeluncomfortable talking to us or feel embarrassed, or they may not want to stand near us.

TALKABOUT Body Language ... Personal appearance

Activity 45 Dressed to impress

Preparation

Photocopy the worksheets, either one for each person or one enlarged to A3 size if you are doing this activity as a group.

Instructions

- Introduce the activity to the group, explaining that they will be thinking about the clothes they wear or an aspect of their appearance that makes them feel good.

- Each group member has a worksheet and thinks about a few things about their appearance that make them feel good and why. This could be a favourite jumper, their hair, a piece of jewellery, etc.

- The group members then share one or two items from their worksheet with everyone else.

Variations

You could have one large worksheet and complete the work as a group. In this case, get each group member to think of one thing about their appearance they like and collate them all on the one sheet.

To step it down, you could focus on one aspect, for example what is everyone's favourite item of clothing?

TALKABOUT Body Language ... Personal appearance

Activity 45 'Dressed to impress' worksheet

Name .... Date ....

Think about what you like about what you wear and the way you look. Remember to think about clothes, hair, accessories.

What makes you feel good and why?

These make me feel good ...	Because ...

TALKABOUT Body Language ... How did I do?

Topic 10 My body language ... how did I do?

Activity 46 Body language ... What am I like? (part 2)

Preparation

Photocopy new assessment sheets. Make sure that you have the completed assessment sheets and target sheets from Activity 6, one for each group member.

Photocopy the certificate of achievement.

Instructions

- Ask the group to consider how they have done over the last few weeks and whether they think they have improved.

- As a group, go through the 'What am I like?' worksheet and ask where they would rate themselves now.

- Then ask the group members to think individually about where they are with their body language skills now and to mark this on their sheet. They may want to sit in different parts of the room to be more private.

- The group facilitator then discusses with each group member how they have rated themselves and they compare this with their original assessment sheet.

- The group members are then given a certificate of achievement.

TALKABOUT Body Language ... How did I do?

Activity 46 'What am I like? (part 2)' worksheet

Name .... Date ....

Body Language ... what am I like at it?

	Never good	Not very good	Quite good	Very good
❶ Eye contact				
❷ Facial expression				
❸ Gesture				
❹ Distance				
❺ Touch				
❻ Fidgeting				
❼ Posture				
❽ Personal appearance				

This page may be photocopied for instructional use only. *Talkabout Second Edition* © Alex Kelly, 2016

TALKABOUT Body Language ... How did I do?

Certificate of Achievement

THIS IS TO CERTIFY THAT

....

HAS COMPLETED TALKABOUT LEVEL 1

BODY LANGUAGE SKILLS

DATE ....

SIGNED ....

👤 Level 2 Talkabout The Way We Talk

Introduction

Objectives To introduce the concept of the way we talk.
To introduce the five aspects of good speaking:
- volume
- rate
- clarity
- intonation
- fluency.

Materials You will need to photocopy several of the activities.
Some of the activity sheets are best enlarged to A3 size.
Some of the activity cards are best laminated.
Some activities are designed to be A5 size to create a fact book on social skills.

This topic will take up to 12 sessions to complete.

Timing

👤 Contents   Page

Activity 1	Listen to me!	134
Activity 2	Why is good speaking important?	137
Activity 3	How do we sound?	141
Activity 4	The way we talk … what am I like? (part 1)	144
Activity 5	My volume	147
Activity 6	My rate	150
Activity 7	My clarity	153
Activity 8	My intonation	155
Activity 9	My fluency	157
Activity 10	The rules for good speaking	159
Activity 11	Learning to do good speaking	161
Activity 12	The way we talk … what am I like? (part 2)	163

TALKABOUT The Way We Talk

Activity 1 Listen to me!

Preparation

Photocopy the handout. This is best laminated if you want to use it again.

You may want to prepare short role plays (modelling) of you and a co-facilitator having a conversation or source video clips of people talking in different ways.

Instructions

- Explain to the group that they are going to watch the facilitators have a conversation. Use a normal scenario, for example, what you did at the weekend. In the conversation, one facilitator should get different aspects of the way they talk wrong, eg talk too loud and too quiet, too fast and too slow, mumble, talk monotonously and hesitate with lots of 'erms' and 'ers' between words. The co-facilitator should keep their speaking appropriate. Below is a sample script which may help.

    F1: (Shouting) Hi Jane!

    F2: Oh hi Sue, you scared me.

    F1: (Whispering) Did you have a good time at the theatre yesterday?

    F2: What?

    F1: (Very fast rate of speech) Did you have a good time at the theatre?

    F2: I'm sorry I can't understand you ...

    F1: (Very slow rate of speech) Did ... you ... have ... a ... good ... time ... at ... the ... theatre?

    F2: Oh yes, it was brilliant. Have you seen the new show yet?

    F1: (Hesitating) Well, um, I erm, I'm not er, sure, I, well, maybe ...

    F2: Well it was really good, the singers were amazing, do you like musicals?

    F1: (Mumbled and unclear) They are OK but I prefer the circus normally.

TALKABOUT The Way We Talk

F2: Sorry, what did you say?

F1: (Monotonous tone) I said they are OK but I prefer the circus normally. I went to see the Russian circus last year and it was the best thing I have ever seen. Anyway, best be going, see you soon.

F2: Oh, OK, bye then.

- Stop and ask the group what did they notice? Was there anything that was not good? They will probably start by commenting on the volume and rate and then may talk about the speaking not being clear enough. You may like to then repeat the model and ask them to look out for anything else. For example, could the co-facilitator understand everything that was said?

- In the second role play, use the same scenario but this time use appropriate speaking.

- You can then show the summary handout and introduce the five aspects of good speaking. Talk about what we mean by each one and that we need to use them all appropriately when talking to people.

- The group members can then put a copy in their fact book, if appropriate.

TALKABOUT The Way We Talk

Activity 1 'Listen to me!' handout

Name .... Date ....

What do we mean by good speaking?

- fluency
- intonation
- clarity
- volume
- rate of speech

TALKABOUT The Way We Talk

Activity 2 Why is good speaking important?

Preparation

Photocopy the cards and stick them back-to-back. Laminate them if you want to use them again.

Photocopy the worksheet.

Instructions

- Explain to the group that you are going to think about all of the reasons why and when good speaking is important. For example:
    - People can understand what we are saying … if we mumble or speak too quickly, people won't be able to understand us.
    - To express ourselves clearly … we need to speak clearly to be able to express our feelings, thoughts and ideas in an appropriate way.
    - To show we are interested … we can use our intonation and volume to show we are interested in what someone is saying.
    - To show how we are feeling … we alter the way we speak to show different emotions, for example, speaking more loudly, quickly and with more varied intonation when we are excited.
    - People will want to talk to us … if we use good speaking, people will feel comfortable and want to talk to us again.
    - To be polite … if we shout or speak very slowly, people may think we are being rude or unkind.

- Use the cards to encourage a discussion. Place the cards text-side down on a table in the middle of the group. You could start by asking what they think the pictures mean and then take it in turns to pick them up and discuss what is on the other side.

- The group members can then complete their worksheet.

TALKABOUT The Way We Talk

Activity 2 'Why is good speaking important?' cards

People can understand what we are saying
If we mumble or speak too quickly, people won't be able to understand us.

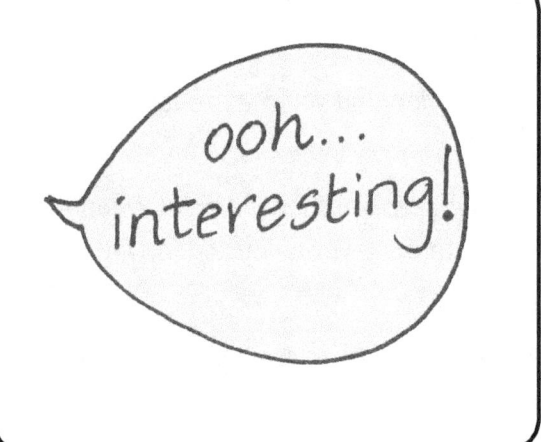

To show we are interested
We can use our intonation and volume to show we are interested in what someone is saying.

People will want to talk to us
If we use good speaking, people will feel comfortable and want to talk to us again.

TALKABOUT The Way We Talk

Activity 2 'Why is good speaking important?' cards

To express ourselves clearly

We need to speak clearly to be able to express our feelings, thoughts and ideas in an appropriate way.

To show how we are feeling

We alter the way we speak to show different emotions, such as speaking more loudly, quickly and with more varied intonation when we are excited.

To be polite

If we shout or speak very slowly, people may think we are being rude or unkind.

TALKABOUT The Way We Talk

Activity 2 'Why is good speaking important?' worksheet

Name .... Date ....

Why is good speaking important?

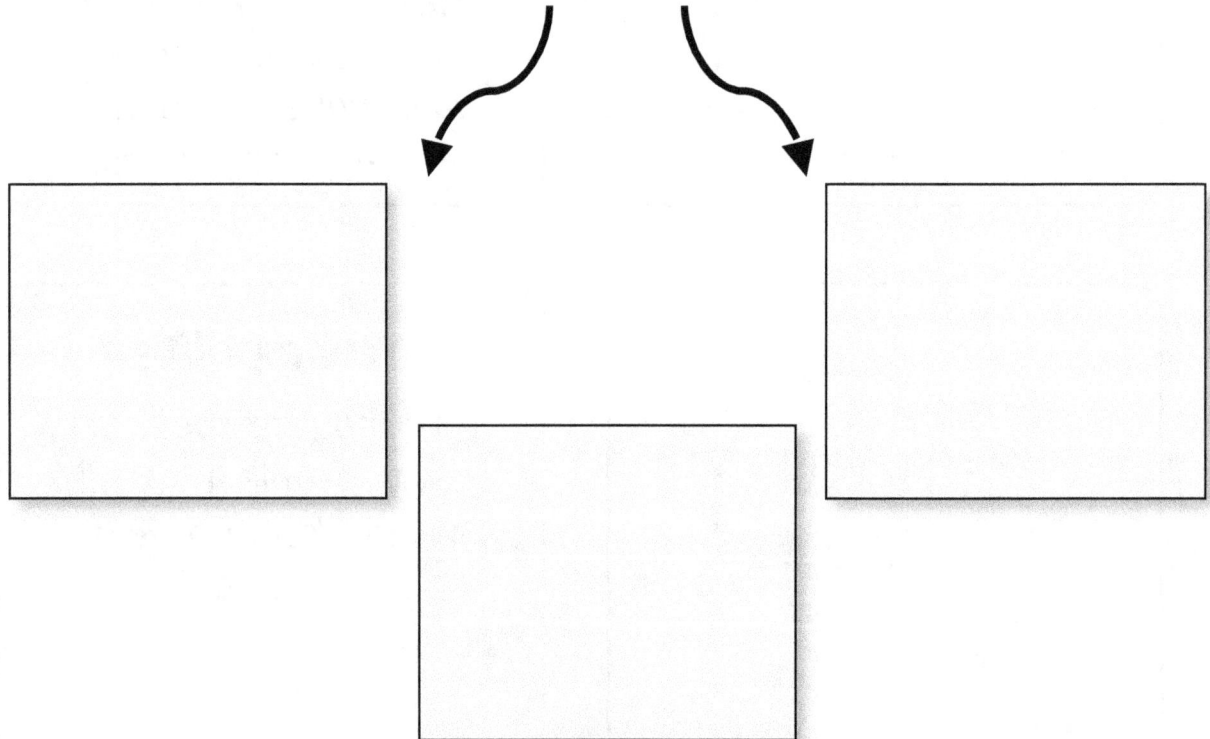

TALKABOUT The Way We Talk

Activity 3 How do we sound?

Preparation

Photocopy and cut out the sentence cards and laminate them if you want to use them again.

Photocopy the worksheet, either one for each group member or one enlarged to A3 size if you are completing the activity as a group.

You will also need the emotions cards from Body Language, Activity 15.

Instructions

- Explain to the group that they are going to be thinking about good speaking today and how it changes with different emotions.

- Place the emotions cards face-down in a pile in the centre of the group. Do the same with the sentence cards. Each group member takes it in turns to select a sentence and an emotion card and then reads the sentence in that way, eg in a sad way or a happy way. You could keep the emotion secret from the group and see if they can guess how the group member is feeling.

- The group then think about how they sounded and what changed in their voice to make them sound that way. You could use the handout from Activity 1 showing the five aspects of speaking to prompt discussion.

- The next group member then repeats this activity until all of the group members have had a turn.

- The group then complete the worksheet either in pairs (you could give one emotion to each pair to complete a sheet) or as a group, deciding on how the five aspects of speaking change to convey different emotions.

Variation

Watch the Talkabout DVD clip on the way we talk (number 17), in which four teenagers say the same thing and show their feelings through the way they say it.

TALKABOUT The Way We Talk

Activity 3 'How do we sound?' cards

✂

| My friend has asked me to go skiing with her at Christmas. I know what Mum is going to say. |

| Sam spoke to Tim and they are both coming round to my house later. I wonder what else they're planning. |

| I hear from Claire that everyone is going out for a drink tonight after work. |

| Richard has just told me that I need to have my work finished and handed in tomorrow. |

| My auntie has given me a new jumper for my birthday. It's red with orange spots. |

| It's raining again today. I am going to stay inside and complete a new puzzle. |

TALKABOUT The Way We Talk

Activity 3 'How do we sound?' worksheet

Name .... Date ....

How do we sound?

When we feel ....

Volume: Quiet — Medium — Loud

Rate: Slow — Medium — Fast

Clarity: Clear — Medium — Mumbled

Intonation: Flat — Medium — Varied

Fluency: Hesitant — Medium — Fluent

TALKABOUT The Way We Talk

Activity 4 The way we talk ... what am I like? (part 1)

Preparation

Photocopy the worksheet, one for each group member. You may like to enlarge one to A3 size to use in the group discussion.

Photocopy a target sheet for each group member.

Instructions

- Remind the group that they are going to be focusing on good speaking for the next few weeks. Therefore, they are going to plan today what they need to work on.

- As a group, go through the 'What am I like?' worksheet, recapping on the different aspects and explaining the rating scale. If group members did not complete this activity in Level 1 Body Language, it is a good idea to get them used to the rating scale first by rating easier skills such as cooking, cycling, getting out of bed in the morning, etc.

- Ask the group members to individually rate the way they talk. They may want to sit in different parts of the room to be more private.

- The group facilitators then discuss with each group member how they have rated themselves. The facilitators then share how they rated that group member on their Talkabout assessment wheel (only the 'way we talk' section), raising awareness of what they need to improve and what they are already doing well.

- The group members can then complete a target sheet for this topic.

TALKABOUT The Way We Talk

Activity 4 'The way we talk … what am I like?' worksheet

Name .... Date ....

The way we talk … what am I like at it?

		Never good	Not very good	Quite good	Very good
❶ Volume					
❷ Rate					
❸ Clarity					
❹ Intonation					
❺ Fluency					

Comments:

This page may be photocopied for instructional use only. *Talkabout Second Edition* © Alex Kelly, 2016

TALKABOUT The Way We Talk

Activity 4 'The way we talk ... what am I like?' target sheet

Name .... Date ....

My plan for the way I talk

 I am good at ...

I need to work on ...

How did I get on?

TALKABOUT The Way We Talk

Activity 5 My volume

Preparation

You will need a large sheet of paper and pens for the group discussion.

Photocopy the worksheets.

You may want to prepare short role plays (modelling) of you and a co-facilitator using good and poor volume in a conversation or source video clips of people talking. You could use the volume clips on the Talkabout DVD as an alternative to the modelling.

Instructions

- Explain to the group that they are going to watch the facilitators have a conversation. Use a normal scenario, for example, talking to each other about what you did at the weekend. In the first role play, one of the group facilitators should talk too loudly while the other person talks normally. Remember not to talk over or interrupt the other facilitator. Stop and ask the group what they noticed. Was there anything that was not good? They will say you spoke too loudly or shouted. You can then ask them what should have happened and they will say you should have spoken more quietly.

- In the second role play, one group facilitator should speak too quietly. Remember to keep all of your body language appropriate, such as not leaning towards the other facilitator. Stop and ask the group what they noticed. Was there anything that was not good? You can then talk about the appropriate volume for a conversation so that people can hear us and don't think we are being rude.

- In the third role play, you can use appropriate volume.

- After each role play, talk about how it makes people appear if they shout or whisper. You could refer to the worksheet in Body Language Activity 7 'Watch my eyes' for ideas. The group members can then complete their worksheets.

Variation

Discuss situations when you can or may need to speak louder, such as at a party or giving a presentation, and when you need to be quieter, such as in a library. You could collect images of different settings and sort them accordingly.

TALKABOUT The Way We Talk

Activity 5 'My volume' worksheet 1

Name .... Date ....

Poor volume

❶ Too loud ...

This means we raise our volume when we are talking to someone and speak too loudly. We may even shout.

If we speak too loudly in a conversation with someone:

The other person may think ....

The other person may feel ....

❷ When might it be OK to be louder?

-
-
-

TALKABOUT The Way We Talk

Activity 5 'My volume' worksheet 2

Name .... Date ....

Poor volume

❶ Too quiet ...

This means we lower our volume when we are talking to someone and speak too quietly. We may even whisper.

If we speak too quietly in a conversation with someone:

The other person may think ....

The other person may feel ....

❷ When might we need to be quieter?

-
-
-

TALKABOUT The Way We Talk

Activity 6 My rate

Preparation

You may need large sheets of paper and pens for the group discussion.

Photocopy the worksheets.

You may want to prepare short role plays (modelling) of you and a co-facilitator having a conversation using a fast or a slow rate of speech, or source video clips of people talking to each other. You could use the rate clips on the Talkabout DVD as an alternative to the modelling.

Instructions

- Explain to the group that they are going to watch the facilitators have a conversation. Use a normal scenario, for example, talking to each other about what you did at the weekend. In the first role play, one of the group facilitators should talk too fast while the other person talks normally. Stop and ask the group what they noticed. Was there anything that was not good? You can ask them what should have happened and they will say you should have spoken more slowly to the other person.

- In the second role play, one of you should speak too slowly with pauses between each word, trying not to change your volume or intonation too much. Stop and ask the group what they noticed. Was there anything that was not good? You can then talk about speaking too slowly and that people may think we are being rude or boring. Talk about an appropriate rate of speech in conversations and suggest that you will try to do better the next time.

- In the third role play, you can use an appropriate rate.

- After each role play, talk about how it makes people appear if they speak too fast or too slowly. You could refer to the worksheet in Body Language Activity 7 'Watch my eyes' for ideas.

- The group members can then complete their worksheets. Discuss and add ideas to them about when your voice may become faster, such as when you are excited or happy, and when it may be slower, such as when you are upset or nervous.

TALKABOUT The Way We Talk

Activity 6 'My rate' worksheet 1

Name .... Date ....

Poor rate

❶ Too fast ...

This means we quicken our rate when we are talking to someone and talk too fast. Our words may become jumbled and people can't understand us.

If we speak too fast in a conversation with someone:

The other person may think ....

The other person may feel ....

❷ Sometimes we talk fast ... why is that?

-
-
-

151

TALKABOUT The Way We Talk

Activity 6 'My rate' worksheet 2

Name .... Date ....

Poor rate

❶ Too slow …

This means we slow down our rate when talking to someone. We may draw out our words or pause between them.

If we speak too slowly when we are talking to someone:

The other person may think ....

The other person may feel ....

❷ Sometimes we talk slowly … why is that?

-
-
-

Activity 7 My clarity

Preparation

You may need large sheets of paper and pens for the group discussion.

Photocopy the worksheet.

You may want to prepare short role plays (modelling) of you and a co-facilitator having a conversation using unclear and clear speech, or source a few video clips of people talking to each other. You could use the clarity clips on the Talkabout DVD as an alternative to the modelling.

Instructions

- Explain to the group that they are going to watch the facilitators have a conversation. Use a normal scenario, for example, talking to each other about what you did at the weekend. In the first role play, one of the group facilitators should mumble a lot while the other person talks normally. Remember not to lower your volume though. Stop and ask the group what they noticed. Was there anything that was not good? You can then ask them what should have happened and they will say you should speak clearly when talking to the other person.

- In the second role play, you can use an appropriate, clear voice.

- After each role play, talk about how it makes people appear if they mumble or speak clearly. You can refer to the worksheet in Body Language Activity 7 'Watch my eyes' for ideas.

- The group members can then complete their worksheet.

Variations

To reinforce the idea of clarity, you could play a 'call and response' game; for example, have a leader who says a sentence or introduces themselves with a fact that the group then repeats back. You could begin by creating a beat, by clapping or tapping your feet, and complete the call and response to this rhythm. When one group member has finished, the next one can have a go, maintaining the beat continuously and remembering to use a good clear voice.

You could also play 'Simon says', remembering that the leader needs to give clear instructions for the group to follow. Take it in turns to be the leader.

TALKABOUT The Way We Talk

Activity 7 'My clarity' worksheet

Name .... Date ....

Poor clarity

❶ Mumbling ...

This means we mumble when we are talking to someone and our words may become unclear and difficult to understand.

If we mumble when we are talking to someone:

The other person may think ....

The other person may feel ....

❷ Clear voice ...

This means we speak clearly when we are talking to people and we are easy to understand.

If we speak clearly when we are talking to someone:

The other person may think ....

The other person may feel ....

TALKABOUT The Way We Talk

Activity 8 My intonation

Preparation

You may need large sheets of paper and pens for the group discussion.

Photocopy the worksheet.

You may want to prepare short role plays (modelling) of you and a co-facilitator having a conversation using poor and good intonation, or source a few video clips of people talking to each other. You could use the intonation clips from the Talkabout DVD as an alternative to the modelling.

Instructions

- Explain to the group that they are going to watch the facilitators have a conversation. Use a normal scenario, for example, talking to each other about what you did at the weekend. In the first role play, one of the group facilitators should use a flat, monotonous intonation while the other person talks normally. Stop and ask the group what they noticed. Was there anything that was not good? They may say you sounded bored or weird but you can ask them what made you sound bored or weird and then you can discuss your flat intonation. Then ask what should have happened and they will say you should sound more excited or lively.

- In the second role play, you could use an overexaggerated intonation. Stop and ask the group what they thought. Was that better?

- In the third role play, you can use appropriate intonation.

- After each role play, talk about how it makes people appear if they use a monotonous or varied intonation. You can refer to the worksheet in Body Language Activity 7 'Watch my eyes' for ideas.

- The group members can then complete their worksheet.

Variation

Create several cards with the same sentence on them but different words stressed, eg I didn't say you had smelly **feet**, I didn't say you had **smelly** feet, I didn't say **you** had smelly feet, I didn't **say** you had smelly feet, **I** didn't say you had smelly feet. The group members take it in turns to select a card and say the sentence, stressing the word in **bold**. The group then discusses how this changes the meaning. The group could then pair up and think of another sentence with a meaning that is changed by stressing different words.

TALKABOUT The Way We Talk

Activity 8 'My intonation' worksheet

Name .... Date ....

Poor intonation

❶ Flat intonation ...

> This means we use the same tone throughout our speech when we are talking to someone. This makes our voice sound flat.
>
> If we use a flat intonation when we are talking to someone:
>
> The other person may think ....
>
> The other person may feel ....

❷ Varied intonation ...

> This means we change our intonation, raising and lowering it while speaking or adding stress to different words, depending on the topic or meaning. (We mustn't vary it too much though!)
>
> If we use varied intonation when we are talking to someone:
>
> The other person may think ....
>
> The other person may feel ....

TALKABOUT The Way We Talk

Activity 9 My fluency

Preparation

You may need large sheets of paper and pens for the group discussion.

Photocopy the worksheet.

You may want to prepare short role plays (modelling) of you and a co-facilitator having a conversation using poor and good fluency, or source a few video clips of people talking to each other. You could use the fluency clips on the Talkabout DVD as an alternative to the modelling.

Instructions

- Explain to the group that they are going to watch the facilitators have a conversation. Use a normal scenario, for example, talking to each other about what you did at the weekend. In the first role play, one of the group facilitators should use a hesitant voice, adding in lots of pauses and 'ums', 'ers' and 'ahs' between words while the other person talks normally. Stop and ask the group what they noticed. Was there anything that was not good? They will probably say you weren't talking clearly or you sounded nervous. In each case, you can ask them how they knew that. You can then ask what should have happened and they will say you should sound more confident. You can then introduce them to the word 'fluent'.

- In the second role play, you can use appropriate fluency.

- After each role play, talk about how it makes people appear if they hesitate or speak fluently. You can refer to the worksheet in Body Language Activity 7, 'Watch my eyes' for ideas.

- The group members can then complete their worksheet.

Variation

To reinforce the idea of fluency, you could play a 'call' game. The group members stand in a circle and the first turns to the second and says 'Hi B', they reply 'Hi A', then the first group member says to the second 'Call C' (the third group member). The second group member then repeats 'Hi C', 'Hi A', 'Call D', continuing until you are back at the beginning. The group members must speak clearly and not hesitate; if they hesitate, they must sit down and are out of the game. You can complete a few rounds until there is a winner. You can change what must be said each round to make it harder.

TALKABOUT The Way We Talk

Activity 9 'My fluency' worksheet

Name .... Date ....

Poor fluency

1 Hesitant voice ...

> This means we hesitate when we are talking to someone and use lots of filler sounds such as 'um' and 'er' between words.
>
> If we hesitate when we are talking to someone:
>
> The other person may think ....
>
> The other person may feel ....

2 Fluent voice ...

> This means we speak confidently and clearly when we are talking to someone with no pauses and hesitations.
>
> If we speak fluently when we are talking to someone:
>
> The other person may think ....
>
> The other person may feel ....

TALKABOUT The Way We Talk

Activity 10   The rules for good speaking

Preparation

Photocopy the handout. Cut them to size if the group members are going to put them in their A5 fact book.

Photocopy the worksheets from Body Language, Activity 11 'Learning to look'.

Instructions

- Explain to the group that you are going to consider the rules for good speaking.

- Ask the group to recap why good speaking is important.

- Then consider the importance of using good speaking to back up what you are saying and help people to understand you and how you are feeling. Discuss the handout as a group.

- Explain that they are going to think about what they can do to use good speaking in their conversations.

- First, ask them to think about what they are currently doing wrong. Are they speaking too quickly or mumbling? Help everyone to describe it by using the sentence 'Sometimes I …'

- Then think about what other people may think or feel about them if they don't do good speaking. Finish the sentence 'Other people may think …'

- Then ask them to think of a sentence that will help them to remember the rule or what they will do. Finish the sentence 'I will try to …'

- Finally, think about why they want to improve this skill. What is the motivation? Is it good to do this because it is the polite thing to do? Or is it because their parents will be proud? Or do they need a reward? This sentence can start with 'This is …' or 'This will mean that …'

- Complete the worksheet from Body Language, Activity 11 'Learning to look', if appropriate.

TALKABOUT The Way We Talk

Activity 10 'The rules for good speaking' handout

Name .... Date ....

Good speaking

What does good speaking mean?

 ✓ Using a clear voice helps people to understand what we are saying and how we are feeling

 ✓ Our voice should match with the content and topic we are talking about

 ✓ We need to remember to use an appropriate volume and rate for a situation – this can vary

 ✓ Remember not to mumble or hesitate so that people can understand you

! Why is this important?

We need to use our voice to help reinforce what we are saying. Remember that our voices will also tell people how we are feeling. For example, when we are nervous, we may speak slower and more quietly and won't use such varied intonation.

If we use inappropriate voices, it can be distracting for the other person and they may not be able to hear or understand us. We may appear either aggressive and rude or passive and nervous.

TALKABOUT The Way We Talk

Activity 11 Learning to do good speaking

Preparation

Photocopy the scenario cards and laminate them if you want to use them again.

Instructions

- Explain to the group that you are going to act out different scenarios and practise using good speaking.

- Ask the group to work in pairs and give each one a scenario. Give them time to create a short role play around that situation.

- The pair must decide who they are in the scenario and then plan the conversation using good speaking, thinking about the five aspects.

- **Note:** make sure that everyone is comfortable taking part in this activity. You may want to check each pair before they perform.

- The pairs then take it in turns to perform their role play to the group. The other group members then comment on whether the speaking was appropriate and clear.

TALKABOUT The Way We Talk

Activity 11 'Learning to do good speaking' cards

You are having a big birthday party tonight and your friend has arrived early to give you a brilliant birthday present.	Your brother or sister is really upset as they have just been told that their pet rabbit has died.
You are having tea with your great uncle who you only see once a year.	You are having an interview for a job at the new clothes shop in town and you really want it.
You're out for dinner with friends and the waiter has brought you the wrong meal. You need to send it back and ask for yours.	You have just met someone new at a party. They seem really friendly and you would like to get to know them better.

TALKABOUT The Way We Talk

Activity 12 The way we talk ... what am I like? (part 2)

Preparation

Photocopy new assessment sheets. Make sure that you have the completed assessment sheets and target sheets from Activity 4, one for each group member.

Photocopy the certificate of achievement.

Instructions

- Ask the group to consider how they have got on over the last few weeks and whether they think they have improved.

- As a group, go through the 'What am I like?' sheet and ask where they would rate themselves now.

- Then ask the group members to think individually about how they would assess their speaking skills now and to mark this on their sheet. They may want to sit in different parts of the room to be more private.

- The group facilitator then discusses with each group member individually how they have rated themselves and they compare this with their original assessment sheet.

- The group members are then given a certificate of achievement.

TALKABOUT The Way We Talk

Activity 12 'What am I like? (part 2)' worksheet

Name .... Date ....

The way we talk ... what am I like at it?

		Never good	Not very good	Quite good	Very good
① Volume					
② Rate					
③ Clarity					
④ Intonation					
⑤ Fluency					

Comments:

TALKABOUT The Way We Talk

Certificate of Achievement

THIS IS TO CERTIFY THAT

....

HAS COMPLETED TALKABOUT LEVEL 2

The Way We Talk

SIGNED .... DATE ....

Level 3 Talkabout Conversations

Introduction

Objectives To introduce the difference between a good conversation and a bad conversation.

To introduce the eight conversational skills:
- listening
- starting a conversation
- taking turns
- asking questions
- answering questions
- being relevant
- repairing
- ending a conversation.

Materials You will need to photocopy several of the activities.

Some of the activity worksheets are best enlarged to A3 size.

Some of the activity cards are best laminated, so that you can use them again.

Some activities are designed to be A5 to create a 'fact book' on social skills.

Timing The topics in Level 3 will take up to 25 sessions to complete.

TALKABOUT Conversations

Contents — page

Topic 1 Talkabout conversations

Activity 1	What are conversational skills?	170
Activity 2	Why worry about conversations?	174
Activity 3	Conversational skills … what am I like? (part 1)	178

Topic 2 Listening

Activity 4	The rules for listening	181
Activity 5	Look and listen	184
Activity 6	Listening time	186

Topic 3 Starting a conversation

Activity 7	Listen to my starters	187
Activity 8	The rules for starting a conversation	189
Activity 9	Starting time	192

Topic 4 Taking turns

| Activity 10 | The rules for turn taking | 193 |
| Activity 11 | Taking time | 196 |

Topic 5 Questions

Activity 12	The rules for asking questions	197
Activity 13	The rules for answering questions	201
Activity 14	Are you open or closed?	205
Activity 15	Question time	208

Topic 6 Being relevant

Activity 16	The rules for relevance	209
Activity 17	Dotty about … dinosaurs	214
Activity 18	Relevance time	216

TALKABOUT Conversations

Topic 7 Repairing

Activity 19	The rules for repairing	217
Activity 20	Repairing time	221

Topic 8 Ending a conversation

Activity 21	Listen to the ending	222
Activity 22	The rules for ending a conversation	225
Activity 23	Conversation critic	228
Activity 24	Ending time	230

Topic 9 How did I do?

Activity 25	Conversational skills … what am I like? (part 2)	231

TALKABOUT Conversations

Topic 1 Talkabout conversations

Activity 1 What are conversational skills?

Preparation

You may need large sheets of paper and pens to write down group discussion ideas.

Photocopy the worksheets and the handout.

Prepare short role plays (modelling) of you and a co-facilitator having a conversation.
You can use the conversation clips on the Talkabout DVD as an alternative to the modelling.

Instructions

- Ask the group to watch you and your co-facilitator have a conversation. Use a normal scenario, for example, talking to each other about what you did at the weekend. In each scenario, one of the group facilitators should do something wrong involving the eight conversational skills, so:

  1. No starter – for example, the person launches into the conversation and surprises the other person.
  2. No listening.
  3. No taking turns.
  4. Asking questions inappropriately.
  5. Poor answering of questions.
  6. Using poor relevance.
  7. Inability to repair – for example, one person uses the wrong name and the other person doesn't correct them.
  8. No ending of the conversation.

- After each scenario, ask the group what they noticed. Was there anything that was not good? Make a note of this, eg 'start the conversation'. In each case, you can ask them what should have happened. You can also talk about how it makes people appear if they don't listen, or don't take turns. You can refer back to the worksheet in Activity 7 in Level 1 Body Language to help generate ideas.

- In the final role play, you should have an appropriate conversation.

- The group members can then complete their worksheets either individually or as a group.

- You can then give each group member the summary handout to look at and add to their fact book, if appropriate.

TALKABOUT Conversations

Activity 1 'What are conversational skills?' worksheet 1

Name …………………………………………………………… Date ………………………

A bad conversation

What do people think?

How do people feel?

TALKABOUT Conversations

Activity 1 'What are conversational skills?' worksheet 2

Name .... Date ....

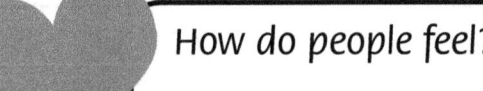

A good conversation

What do people think?

How do people feel?

TALKABOUT Conversations

Activity 1 'What are conversational skills?' handout

Name ....

Date ....

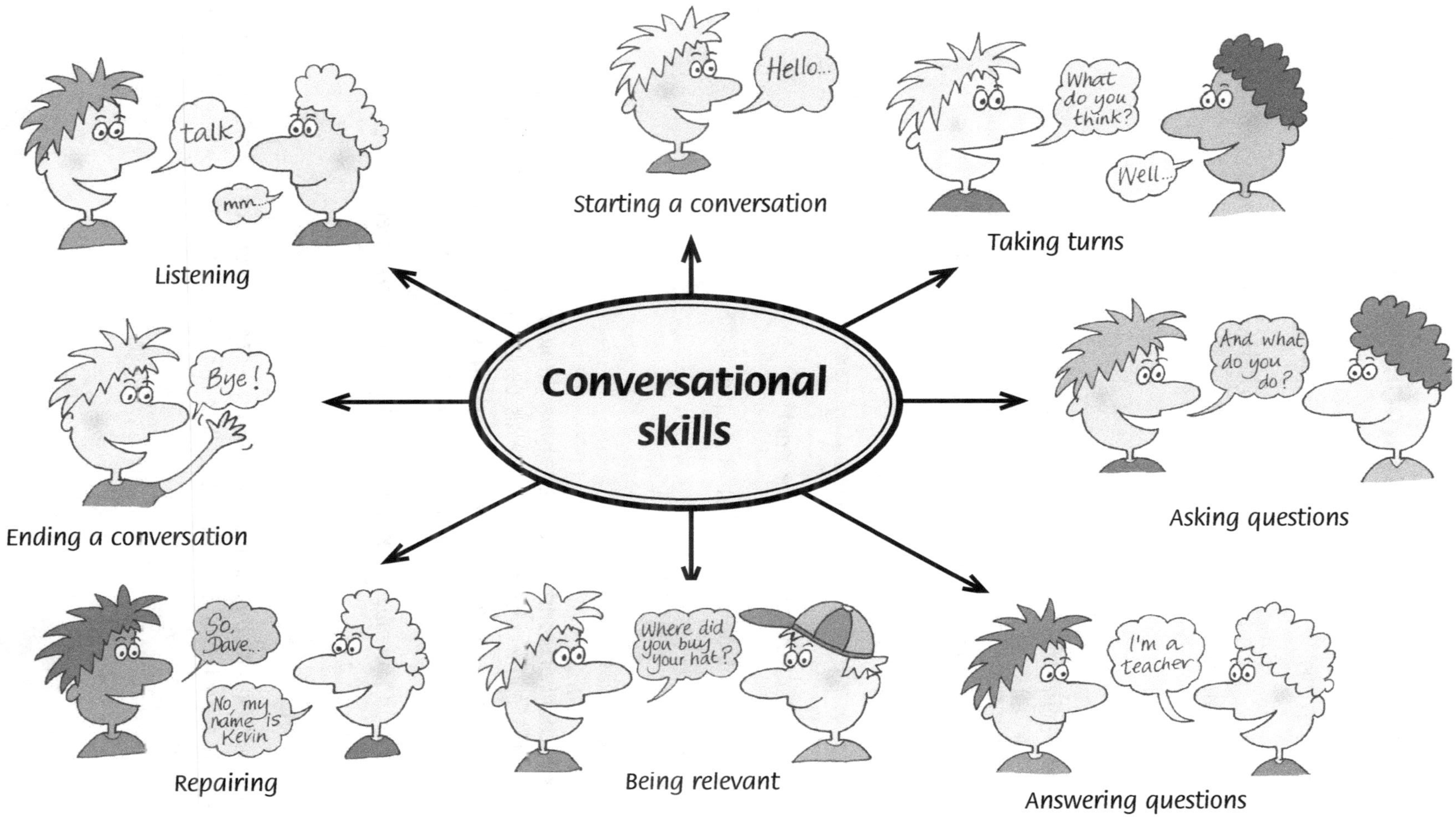

Conversational skills

- Starting a conversation
- Taking turns
- Asking questions
- Answering questions
- Being relevant
- Repairing
- Ending a conversation
- Listening

TALKABOUT Conversations

Activity 2 Why worry about conversations?

Preparation

Photocopy and cut out the cards and stick them back-to-back. Laminate them if you want to use them again.

Photocopy the worksheet.

Instructions

- Explain to the group that you are going to think about all of the reasons why it is important to be good at conversations. For example, to:

    o   make friends

    o   show people we are interested in them

    o   find out things we need or want

    o   get a job or work with other people

    o   express ourselves

    o   be polite.

- You could demonstrate these reasons through different role plays (modelling) or you could use the cards to elicit some discussion. If you are using the cards, place them text-side down. You could start by asking what they think the pictures mean and then take it in turns to pick up the cards and discuss what is on the other side.

- The group members can then complete their worksheet.

Variation

Ask the group members to think about a recent conversation they have had. Why did they need to have this conversation or talk to that person? Was it for one of the above reasons or something else?

TALKABOUT Conversations

Activity 2 'Why worry about conversations?' cards

To make friends
It is easier to make friends if we can talk to people easily. We can also have fun talking to them!

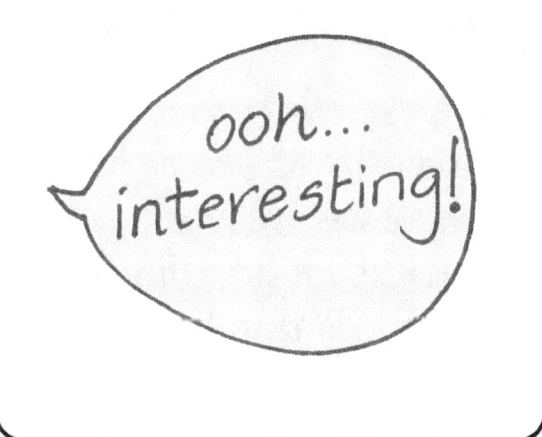

To show people we are interested
We let people know we are interested in them by talking to them. We may ask questions or talk to them about their feelings.

To find out things we need or want
We use our good conversational skills to ask people for things we may need or want.

Activity 2 'Why worry about conversations?' cards

To get a job or work with other people

People with good conversational skills find it easier to get work and to work with others.

To express ourselves

We use our conversational skills to let people know how we are feeling and what we are thinking. This will also help build relationships.

To be polite

People like us to be good at having a conversation. They like us to take turns and listen and then ask good questions.

TALKABOUT Conversations

Activity 2 'Why worry about conversations?' worksheet

Name .... Date ....

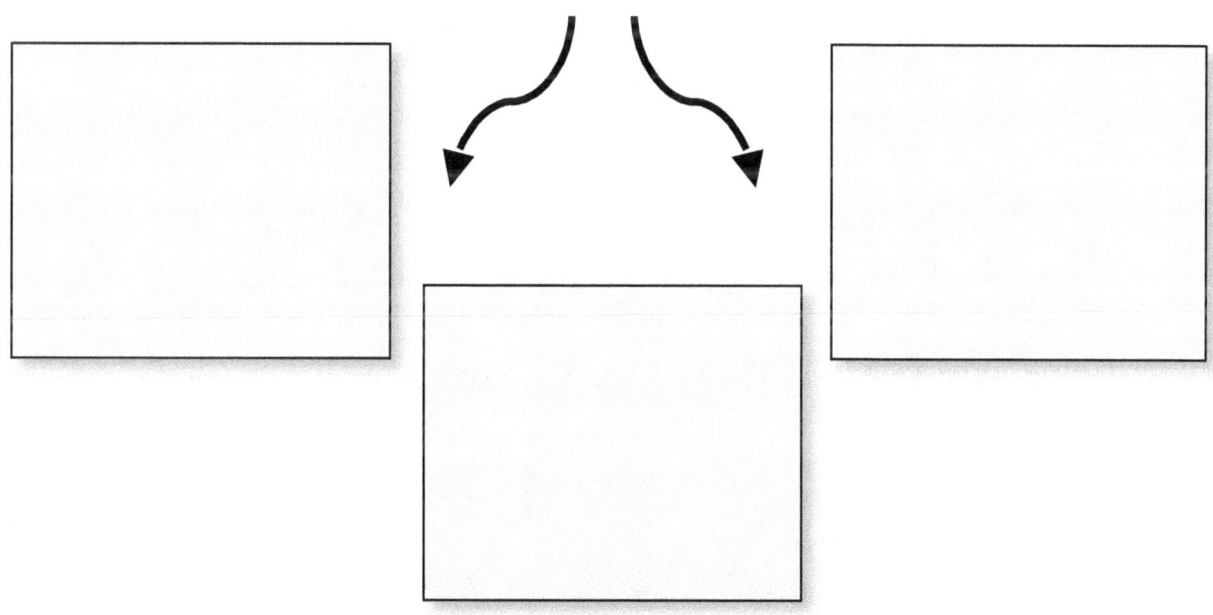

Why is it important to be good at conversations?

TALKABOUT Conversations

Activity 3 Conversational skills ... what am I like? (part 1)

Preparation

Photocopy the assessment sheet, one for each group member. You may like to enlarge one to A3 size to use in a group discussion.

Photocopy a target sheet for each group member.

Instructions

- Remind the group that they are going to be focusing on conversational skills for the next few sessions. Therefore, they are going to plan today what they need to work on.

- As a group, go through the 'What am I like?' assessment sheet, explaining the different behaviours and the rating scale. You may need to remind the group how to use the rating scale by rating easier everyday skills, such as cooking, cycling, getting out of bed in the morning, etc.

- Then ask the group members to think individually about where they are with their conversational skills. They may want to sit in different parts of the room for this to be more private.

- The group facilitator(s) then discuss with each group member how they have rated themselves. The facilitators then share how they rated that group member in their Talkabout assessment (only the 'conversation skills' section of the wheel), raising awareness of what they need to improve on and what they are already doing well.

- The group members can then complete a target sheet for the conversational skills topic.

TALKABOUT Conversations

Activity 3 'Conversational skills … what am I like?' assessment sheet

Name .... Date ....

Conversational skills … what am I like?

	Never good	Not very good	Quite good	Very good
① Listening				
② Starting a conversation				
③ Taking turns				
④ Asking questions				
⑤ Answering questions				
⑥ Being relevant				
⑦ Repairing				
⑧ Ending a conversation				

TALKABOUT Conversations

Activity 3 'Conversational skills ... what am I like?' target sheet

Name ………………………………………………………….. Date ……………………..

My conversational skills plan

| 😊 I am good at ... | ✓ |

| I need to work on ... | How did I get on? |

180   Ⓟ This page may be photocopied for instructional use only. *Talkabout Second Edition* © Alex Kelly, 2016

TALKABOUT Conversations ... Listening

Topic 2 Listening

Activity 4 The rules for listening

Preparation

You will need a large sheet of paper and pens to write down the group discussion ideas.

Photocopy the worksheet and the handout.

You may want to prepare short role plays (modelling) of you and a co-facilitator having a conversation, or source a few video clips of people talking to each other and showing good and poor listening. You could use the listening clips on the Talkabout DVD as an alternative to the modelling.

Instructions

- Explain that the group members are going to watch the facilitators have a conversation. Use a normal scenario, for example, talking to each other about what you did at the weekend. In the first scenario, one of the group facilitators should not listen to the other person. You can break this down into several role plays to demonstrate the key skills: looking, good posture, appropriate facial expression, making the right noises, asking questions, and saying something relevant. Stop and ask the group each time what they noticed. Was there anything that was not good? How did it make them appear? You can then ask them what should have happened.

- In the final role play, you can show appropriate listening.

- Write down a list of all the things they think it is important to do to show someone you are listening.

- The group members can then complete their worksheet and discuss the rules on the handout.

Note on 'Learning to ...': now consider whether any of the group members need to complete a 'Learning to ...' worksheet on listening (a plan of action). If appropriate, refer to Activity 11 'Learning to look' in Level 1 Body Language for instructions and the worksheet.

TALKABOUT Conversations ... Listening

Activity 4 'The rules of listening' worksheet

Name .... Date ....

Poor listening

❶ Poor listening ...

This means we do not listen to someone when they are talking to us. We may not look at them or use appropriate facial expressions or body language. We may then ask inappropriate questions or say something that is not relevant.

If we don't listen to someone when they are talking to us:

The other person may think ....

The other person may feel ....

❷ How can we show that we are listening?

....

....

....

....

TALKABOUT Conversations ... Listening

Activity 4 'The rules of listening' handout

Name .... Date ....

Listening

What is good listening?

- ✓ Good listening means we should try to use good eye contact

- ✓ We should also try to use appropriate facial expressions

- ✓ We should try to use an open posture or lean forwards

- ✓ We should comment on what they are saying and ask appropriate questions

Why is this important?

It is polite to listen to people when they are talking to us. Listening to people will help us to make friends because people like people who listen to them.

If we don't listen, people may think we are rude and not want to talk to us.

TALKABOUT Conversations ... Listening

Activity 5 Look and listen

Preparation

Create some space in the room so that the group members can work in groups of three.

Photocopy the worksheet.

Instructions

- Ask the group to divide into groups of three. If this is not possible, have a group of four or ask one of the facilitators to join a group. Ideally, they will need one person to talk, one person to listen and one person to observe.

- Ask each group to prepare something to talk about. For example, they may like to talk about their favourite holiday or what they enjoy doing in the evenings. If some of the group members are struggling to think about a topic, make a list for the whole group to work from.

- Explain that they will take it in turns to be in each role: talker, listener and observer. The observer will watch the person listening and will note in particular their eye contact, facial expression, posture and use of commenting.

- At the end of the conversation, the observer feeds back what they thought and they then agree on what kind of smiley face they should draw (green, orange or red).

- Repeat the activity until everyone has had a go.

- This activity can be repeated a second time, so that they can improve on any areas that were not good.

- Then try swapping the groups around, so that they work with different people.

- Finally, each group can complete their worksheet.

TALKABOUT Conversations ... Listening

Activity 5 'Look and listen' worksheet

Name .... Date ....

1 How did I do?

Name	Good eye contact	Good facial expression	Good posture	Good commenting
❶	○	○	○	○
❷	○	○	○	○
❸	○	○	○	○

2 How did I do?

Name	Good eye contact	Good facial expression	Good posture	Good commenting
❶	○	○	○	○
❷	○	○	○	○
❸	○	○	○	○

TALKABOUT Conversations ... Listening

Activity 6 Listening time ... the zoo game and more

Additional listening games

- **Zoo game.** Ask each person to choose an animal. The group facilitator then reads a story that incorporates all of the animals chosen. The group members need to listen to the story and when they hear their animal, they have to stand up and sit back down again. If they hear the word 'zoo', they all stand up and sit down. This activity can be varied by changing the topic and key word, eg to 'food' or 'shopping'. You can also vary the actions so that everyone has to 'clap' or 'turn around' when they hear a particular word.

- **Fruit salad.** Everyone chooses a fruit and one chair is removed from the circle. One person stands in the middle of the circle and calls out two fruits. These two 'fruits' change places and the person in the middle tries to sit in one of their seats. The person left standing repeats the process. If someone calls out 'fruit salad', everyone has to change seats.

- **Change places if ...** The group leader asks people to change places if they like chocolate, have brown hair, watched television last night, etc. Try using a parachute and, standing in a circle, make the parachute go up and down. Call out the command just before the parachute goes up and they then change places quickly before the parachute comes back down.

- **I went to the market.** The first person says 'I went to market and bought a ...' The next person has to repeat the first person's object and then adds their own. You can add actions or mimes and can also change the topic, for example, 'I went on holiday and took/saw ...'

- **Simon says.** The group leader says 'Simon says ...' and does an action or requests an action (eg 'stand up'). The group members only follow the action if the leader says 'Simon says ...' before the action. If the group leader says 'Sit down' without saying 'Simon says', the group members should not do it and, if they do, they are out of the game.

- **Tell a story.** One person starts a story by saying 'Once upon a time ...' Each group member then adds a sentence to create a story. One of the group facilitators can write down the story and read it back at the end of the game.

TALKABOUT Conversations ... Starting a conversation

Topic 3 Starting a conversation

Activity 7 Listen to my starters

Preparation

You may need large sheets of paper and pens to write down the group discussion ideas.

Photocopy the worksheet.

You may want to prepare short role plays (modelling) of you and a co-facilitator starting a conversation, or source a few video clips of people starting conversations. You could use the clip on starting a conversation on the Talkabout DVD as an alternative to the modelling.

Instructions

- Explain that the group members are going to watch the facilitators have a conversation. Use a normal scenario, for example, talking to each other about what you did at the weekend. In the first scenario, one of the group facilitators should attempt to start a conversation by walking up but then not saying anything and, after a while, walking away. Ask the group what they noticed. Was there anything not good? They will say you didn't say anything. After each role play, ask the group how it made the person appear.

- In the next role play, the group facilitator starts the conversation by saying 'Hello' appropriately but walks up and stands too close to the co-facilitator. They may say 'Hello' into the person's back or neck and make them jump. Ask the group what went wrong. They will say you can't stand so close or you need to get your body language right too.

- In the third role play, the first group facilitator tries again to begin a conversation but this time by saying 'Hello' and then asking a personal question such as 'So how much do you get paid?' Ask the group if that was better. They will say you need to say something appropriate. Ask what you could say and then suggest that you will do better the next time.

- In the final role play, you can start a conversation appropriately.

- The group can then complete their worksheet. You could also refer to the worksheet in Activity 7 in Level 1 Body Language.

TALKABOUT Conversations ... Starting a conversation

Activity 7 'Listen to my starters' worksheet

Name .... Date ....

Poor starters

❶ Poor greeting ...

This means we may not say anything or we say something inappropriate when starting a conversation, such as asking a personal question.

If we don't greet someone appropriately when starting a conversation:

The other person may think ....

The other person may feel ....

❷ Poor body language ...

This means we stand behind someone, or with our body facing away from them, when attempting to start a conversation. We may not look at them.

If we use poor body language when starting a conversation:

The other person may think ....

The other person may feel ....

TALKABOUT Conversations ... Starting a conversation

Activity 8 The rules for starting a conversation

Preparation

You will need a large sheet of paper and pens to write down the discussion ideas.

Photocopy the worksheet, enough for one per pair.

Print out the handout and cut the copies to size if the group members are going to put them in their A5 fact book.

Instructions

- Explain to the group that you are going to consider the different ways in which you can start a conversation.

- Ask the group to suggest all of the different ways in which they could start a conversation. Write down these ideas on a large sheet of paper.

- Introduce the worksheet and explain that there are five main ways we start a conversation, then talk about each one. Ask the group to work in pairs to complete the worksheet. For each of the five areas, they must add an example from the previous discussion and then one different example of their own.

- The pairs then share their ideas with the group. You could add new ideas and examples from the worksheets to the large sheet of paper. Keep this safe as you may like to refer back to it in later sessions.

- Distribute the handout and discuss what it says. Talk about the rules for starting a conversation and what we need to remember.

Note on 'Learning to ...': now consider whether any of the group members need to complete a 'Learning to ...' worksheet on starting a conversation (a plan of action). If appropriate, refer to Activity 11 'Learning to look' in Level 1 Body Language for instructions and the worksheet.

TALKABOUT Conversations ... Starting a conversation

Activity 8 'The rules for starting a conversation' worksheet

Name .... Date ....

Summary of starters

Can you think of two examples for each one?

1 Asking a question

2 Requesting or giving something

3 Commenting on the environment

4 General greeting

5 Personal remark

TALKABOUT Conversations ... Starting a conversation

Activity 8 'The rules for starting a conversation' handout

Name .... Date ....

Starting a conversation
What are good starters?

 ✓ We need to face someone when we want to start a conversation and look at them

 ✓ We should use an appropriate greeting such as 'Hello' or 'Good morning'

 ✓ We could ask a question or make a comment such as 'What a sunny day!'

 ✓ We need to use good speaking as well, so that someone can hear and understand us clearly

Why is this important?

It is important to start a conversation appropriately to be polite and so that other people will want to talk to us. It will allow us to have a conversation and to express ourselves. It will also make us appear friendly. If we don't start a conversation well, people may think we are rude and won't want to talk to us.

TALKABOUT Conversations ... Starting a conversation

Activity 9 Starting time ... 'Pass the greeting' and more

Additional activities for starting a conversation

- **Pass the greeting.** Write down each of the five ways to start a conversation on separate cards. Place the cards in a pile face-down in the middle of the group. The first group member chooses who they would like to start a conversation with and selects a card to determine how they should do this. They then start their conversation.

  Continue until everyone has had a turn starting a conversation. Discuss how it went. Alternatively, you could make the cards into a dice by sticking them on an empty tissues box and then roll the dice to choose the starter. On the sixth side, add 'you choose'.

- **Musical starters.** Divide the group into two groups of the same size. One group stands in a tight circle facing outwards and the other group walks around this circle until the group facilitator shouts 'Stop!' They should stop, facing a group member in the inner circle who they must then start a conversation with. While the group members are walking around the circle, the group facilitator will say how to start the conversation, eg begin with a comment about the environment.

- **Starting up Sam.** Ask the group to divide into pairs. Decide on a few scenarios such as meeting someone at a party, seeing your friend in town, visiting your granny, going for a job interview. Give each pair a scenario and ask them to create a short role play showing starting a conversation in that context. Each pair must decide who they are, what the conversation will be about and what would be an appropriate way of starting that conversation.

  Make sure that everyone feels comfortable and check all of the role plays before the pairs perform them to the group. The pairs then perform and the group members discuss whether they think the greeting is appropriate for that setting.

TALKABOUT Conversations ... Taking turns

Topic 4 Taking turns

Activity 10 The rules for turn taking

Preparation

You may need large sheets of paper and pens for the group discussion.

Photocopy the worksheet and the handout.

You may want to prepare short role plays (modelling) of you and a co-facilitator having a conversation, or source a few video clips of people talking to each other. You could use the turn-taking clips on the Talkabout DVD as an alternative to the modelling.

Instructions

- Explain that the group members are going to watch the facilitators have a conversation. In the first scenario, both facilitators say 'Hello' and then nothing else. They continue to look at each other while there is a long silence; they then both say 'Goodbye'. Stop and ask the group what they noticed. Was there anything not good about it? They will say you didn't say anything or you didn't talk. Suggest that you will do better the next time and you will say something. After each role play, ask the group how it made the people appear.

- In the next role play, both group facilitators say 'Hello' and then both begin talking. They continue to talk at the same time for the whole conversation before both saying 'Goodbye'. (**Note:** this takes a few practices to do well!) Ask the group if that was better. They will say that you both talked at once, so suggest that you will do better next time.

- In the third role play, one group facilitator will dominate the conversation. Both facilitators say 'Hello' and then one begins talking non-stop. They may ask the other person a question but then won't let them answer. The second facilitator will try to say things but not be allowed. Both then say 'Goodbye'. Stop and ask the group if that was better. The group will say you need to let the other person speak.

- In the final role play, you can take turns appropriately.

- The group then complete their worksheet. You could also refer to the worksheet from Activity 7 in Level 1 Body Language.

- Distribute the handout and discuss what it says. Talk about the rules around turn taking in a conversation and what we need to remember.

Note on 'Learning to ...': now consider whether any of the group members need to complete a 'Learning to ...' worksheet on taking turns (a plan of action). If appropriate, refer to Activity 11 'Learning to look' in Level 1 Body Language for instructions and the worksheet.

TALKABOUT Conversations ... Taking turns

Activity 10 'The rules for turn taking' worksheet

Name .... Date ....

Poor turn taking

❶ Talking at once ...

This means we may both speak at the same time. This means that we can't hear each other or respond appropriately.

If we talk at the same time in a conversation:

The other person may think ....

The other person may feel ....

❷ Uneven turns ...

This means one person in the conversation talks too much and doesn't let the other person have a fair turn. They may even not let them talk at all.

If one person talks too much in a conversation:

The other person may think ....

The other person may feel ....

TALKABOUT Conversations ... Taking turns

Activity 10 'The rules for turn taking' handout

Name .... Date ....

Turn taking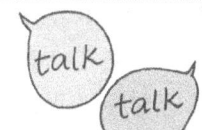

What does good turn taking mean?

 ✓ In a conversation, we want to have enough time to be able to say what we want

 ✓ We also need to give the other person time to talk

 ✓ When someone else is talking, we should keep quiet and let them have their turn

 ✓ We can use eye contact to show it is the other person's time to talk

Why is this important?

It is important to take turns in a conversation appropriately to be polite and so that everyone has a chance to talk. It will allow us to have a good conversation and other people will want to talk to us again. If we don't take turns well, people may think we are rude and may not want to talk to us.

TALKABOUT Conversations ... Taking turns

Activity 11 Taking time ... 'Pass the mic' and more

Additional activities for taking turns

- **Pass the mic.** The group members sit in a circle with a microphone in the middle (this could be any object if you don't have a microphone). They are given a topic to discuss, such as their favourite holiday or meal, but they can only speak when they have the microphone. The group will have to decide how they signal that they want to speak and if someone is talking too much.

- **I went to the Moon.** The group members sit in a circle. The group facilitator thinks of a rule in their head, such as things beginning with 'A', or things that have wheels. They then begin by saying 'I went to the Moon and I took ...' and say something that fits their rule. Then go around the circle taking it in turns to say 'I went to the Moon and I took ...', adding something to try to guess the rule. After each guess, the group facilitator says 'yes' or 'no' depending on whether that is something they can take. The game continues until the rule has been guessed correctly. Someone else in the group can then have a turn to decide on a rule.

- **I went to the market.** This activity encourages the group to take turns and listen to what the group members have said before them. The first person says 'I went to the market and I bought an egg'. The second person says 'I went to the market and I bought an egg and a magazine'. The third says 'I went to the market and I bought an egg, a magazine and some biscuits', and so on, until you have been round the group a couple of times. Ask the rest of the group to help if someone gets stuck.

- **Taking turns Toni.** Ask the group to divide into pairs. Decide on a few scenarios such as at a party, at work, seeing your grandparents, etc. Give each pair a scenario and ask them to prepare a short role play showing good turn taking. Each pair must decide who they are, and what the conversation will be about and practise using good turn taking. The pairs then perform their role plays and the group members discuss whether they think the turn taking was appropriate for that setting.

TALKABOUT Conversations ... Questions

Topic 5 Questions

Activity 12 The rules for asking questions

Preparation

You may need large sheets of paper and pens to write down the group discussion ideas.

Photocopy the worksheet and the handout.

You may want to prepare short role plays (modelling) of you and a co-facilitator having a conversation, or source a few video clips of people talking to each other and asking questions. You could use the asking questions clips on the Talkabout DVD as an alternative to the modelling.

Instructions

- Explain to the group that they are going to watch the facilitators have a conversation. Use the scenario where you have just met and want to find out more about each other. In the first role play, the facilitators have a conversation but one doesn't ask any questions while the other continues to ask questions to find out more about them. The facilitator who is asking questions may pause at times as they expect to be asked a question too. Ask the group what they noticed. Was there anything not good? Did both facilitators find out lots of facts about each other? They will say only one did because the other didn't ask any questions. That facilitator suggests they will do better the next time and will ask some questions.

- In the next role play, use the same scenario but, this time, the facilitator who didn't ask questions in the first role play now asks questions but they are inappropriate. For example, they may ask if they are married, and if not why, what do they earn, do they have any tattoos, where do they buy their underwear from, etc. The other facilitator does their best to answer but may look embarrassed or uncomfortable and will continue to ask appropriate questions. Ask the group if that was better. They will say 'no' because the questions were inappropriate.

- In the third role play, change the topic slightly by saying you want to find out about each other's weekend. Ask a couple of questions appropriately at the beginning and then one group facilitator will dominate the conversation by continually asking questions too quickly. These initially may be about the other facilitator's weekend but could then switch to the weather or their new hair cut or outfit. Ask the group if that was better. They will say that you asked too many questions and need to let the other person ask some. Suggest that you will do better the next time.

TALKABOUT Conversations ... Questions

Instructions (continued)

- In the final role play, you can ask questions about each other's weekend appropriately.

- After each role play, ask the group how did it make the people appear?

- The group can then complete their worksheet. You could also refer to the worksheet from Activity 7 in Level 1 Body Language.

- Distribute the handout and discuss what it says. Talk about the rules around asking questions in a conversation and what we need to remember.

TALKABOUT Conversations ... Questions

Activity 12 'The rules for asking questions' worksheet

Name .... Date ....

Poor asking

❶ Asking the wrong questions ...

This means we may ask questions that are not relevant to the topic of conversation or ask questions that are not appropriate for that person.

If we ask the wrong questions:

The other person may think ....

The other person may feel ....

❷ Asking the wrong number of questions ...

This means we may ask too many questions and overload the other person, or we may not ask any questions at all.

If we ask too many questions or none at all:

The other person may think ....

The other person may feel ....

TALKABOUT Conversations... Questions

Activity 12 'The rules for asking questions' handout

Name …………………………………………………………… Date ……………………………

Asking questions
What does good asking mean?

 ✓ In conversations we want to be able to ask questions to find things out

 ✓ We need to ask appropriate questions, relevant to the topic and the other person

 ✓ We need to make sure we ask questions but that we don't ask too many

 ✓ We can ask open or closed questions depending on how much detail we want

❗ Why is this important?

It is important to take turns in a conversation appropriately to be polite and so that everyone has a chance to talk. It will allow us to have a good conversation and other people will want to talk to us again. If we don't take turns well, people may think we are rude and may not want to talk to us.

TALKABOUT Conversations... Questions

Activity 13 The rules for answering questions

Preparation

You may need large sheets of paper and pens to write down the group discussion ideas.

Photocopy the worksheet and the handout.

You may want to prepare short role plays (modelling) of you and a co-facilitator having a conversation, or source a few video clips of people talking to each other and answering questions. You could use the answering questions clips on the Talkabout DVD as an alternative to the modelling.

Instructions

- Explain to the group that they are going to watch the facilitators have a conversation. Use a normal scenario, for example, talking to each other about what you did at the weekend. In the first role play, one facilitator will ask questions appropriately about the weekend but the other doesn't answer. They may not say anything at all or they may say or talk about something different. Stop and ask the group what they noticed. Was there anything not good about it? They will say you didn't answer any of the questions. Suggest that you will do better the next time and that you will answer the other person.

- In the next role play, the group facilitator will answer the questions but inappropriately. For example, they may say something too personal or won't answer the questions properly, eg 'What's your favourite pizza?', 'Well I just love a chicken burger'. Ask the group if that was better and they will say 'no' because you gave strange answers or said inappropriate things. Talk about how answers should be relevant to the question and then suggest that you will do better the next time.

- In the third role play, the group facilitator will answer the questions appropriately but give either too much detail or not enough. The other facilitator may ask 'Did you have a nice weekend?' 'Yes.' 'Did you go anywhere nice?' 'Yes.' 'Where did you go?' 'Go-karting.' Later on, the group facilitator may then give an answer that is far too long and detailed and the other facilitator will look bored. Stop and ask the group if that was better. The group will say 'no' because you didn't say enough or you said too much and the other person was bored. Talk about how we have to keep the length of our answers appropriate to both the setting and the person.

- In the final role play, the questions are answered appropriately.

- After each role play, ask the group how it made the people appear.

Instructions (continued)

- The group can then complete their worksheet. You could also refer to the worksheet from Activity 7 in Level 1 Body Language.

- Distribute the handout and discuss what it says. Talk about the rules for answering a question in a conversation and what we need to remember.

Note on 'Learning to ...': now consider whether any of the group members need to complete a 'Learning to ...' worksheet on asking or answering questions (a plan of action). If appropriate, refer to Activity 11 'Learning to look' in the body language section for instructions and the worksheet.

TALKABOUT Conversations ... Questions

Activity 13 'The rules for answering questions' worksheet

Name .... Date ....

Poor answering

❶ Answering inappropriately ...

> This means we answer a question we have been asked but our answer is not relevant or gives inappropriate information such as something too personal.
>
> If we answer questions inappropriately in a conversation:
>
> The other person may think ....
>
> The other person may feel ....

❷ Answering with inappropriate detail ...

> This means we answer a question that we have been asked but either don't give enough detail, or just say 'Yes' or our answer is too long.
>
> If our answers are too long or short in a conversation:
>
> The other person may think ....
>
> The other person may feel ....

Activity 13 'The rules for answering questions' handout

Name .... Date ....

Answering questions ???
What does good answering mean?

✓ In a conversation we like to answer questions to share information and give our ideas

✓ We must remember to listen to the question and then make our answers relevant

✓ If we are asked a closed question, our answer should be short and normally just 'Yes' or 'No'

✓ If we are asked an open question, we can give more detail but be careful not to give too much information and bore the other person

! Why is this important?

It is important to answer questions appropriately in a conversation to be polite and to help to get to know each other.

If we don't answer questions well, people may think we are rude or get bored by our answers and may not want to talk to us.

TALKABOUT Conversations ... Questions

Activity 14 Are you open or closed?

Preparation

You will need some small pieces of paper and pens for the group discussion.

Photocopy the headings cards and the sentences. Laminate them if you want to use them again and then cut them out.

Photocopy the worksheet.

Instructions

- Explain to the group that there are two different types of question that people ask. One is a closed question where the answer is very short and usually just 'Yes' or 'No'. These are good for getting answers and information quickly.

- The second type is an open question. These are questions where the answer can be longer, where we give more detail and we can expand, giving longer explanations. These are good for getting lots of information and used when getting to know someone, or understanding something or when we are really interested in a topic.

- Place the two headings in the middle of the group and the sentences in a pile face-down. The group members take it in turns to select a sentence and ask it to the person on their left who then answers. They then decide whether that was an open or a closed question and place it under the appropriate heading. Continue until all of the sentences are sorted.

- Next, the group members can spend some time thinking up their own ideas and examples of open and closed questions. They could write them down and add them under the headings.

- Finally, complete the worksheet, either as a group or in pairs. Read about what we mean by a closed question and then think about when you may use them, eg when you need information quickly, when you only need to know one thing, etc. Then think about open questions. When might we use those? For example, when we want to hear a story, or know someone's ideas or opinions or when getting to know someone.

TALKABOUT Conversations ... Questions

Activity 14 'Are you open or closed?' cards

| Open questions |

| Closed questions |

| Can you open that window please? |

| What is your favourite meal? |

| Would you like mayonnaise on that? |

| What is the best holiday you have been on? |

| Do you like swimming? |

| Where do you live? |

| Do you own a car? |

| What pets do you have at home? |

TALKABOUT Conversations ... Questions

Activity 14 'Are you open or closed?' worksheet

Name .... Date ....

Open and closed questions

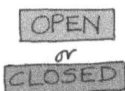 ### Closed questions

The answer to a closed question is short and normally just a yes or a no. They are good when ...

-
-
-

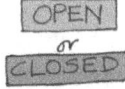 ### Open questions

The answer to an open question is normally much longer. We can expand and give lots more detail and information.
They are good when ...

-
-
-

TALKABOUT Conversations ... Questions

Activity 15 Question time ... 'twenty questions' and more

Additional activities for asking and answering questions

- **Twenty questions.** The group members sit in a circle and are each given three small slips of paper. On one they write an animal, on another they write a food and on the third they write an object. They then fold each piece of paper and put them in a hat or bowl. The group then take it in turns to pick out a piece of paper and tell the group whether it is an animal, a food or an object. The group then have twenty questions to guess what it is but the person with the paper can only answer yes or no. The person who guesses correctly wins!

- **Question time.** Divide the group into smaller groups of two or three. Ask them to think about two things that they don't already know about the other two people and note these down. They then take it in turns for one to be the observer and the other two to have a short conversation, asking and answering questions to find out the two facts. They then switch roles so that all three have had a chance to be the observer. The whole group then discuss how it went. Did everyone ask good questions? Did people use a mix of open and closed questions and how did this go?

- **Yes/no game.** One group member starts by sitting in the middle of the group. The rest of the group then take it in turns to ask them questions. These could range from 'Do you like chocolate?' to 'Have you got brothers and sisters?'. The person in the middle must answer the questions but cannot say 'yes' or 'no'. As soon as they do, they are out of the game and the next group member sits in the middle.

- **Asking Alex.** Get the group to divide into pairs. Decide on a few scenarios such as meeting someone new, going for an interview, seeing a friend who you haven't seen for a year. Choose scenarios where lots of questions will be asked. Give each pair a scenario and then 5 to 10 minutes to prepare a short role play. They must decide who they are in the role play and questions they think would be relevant. You may even like to stipulate that each role play must have a minimum number of open and closed questions. The pairs then perform their role plays for the group and afterwards discuss how they got on with their questions and answers.

TALKABOUT Conversations ... Being relevant

Topic 6 Being relevant

Activity 16 The rules for relevance

Preparation

You may need large sheets of paper and pens to write down the group discussion ideas.

Photocopy the worksheets and the handout.

You may want to prepare short role plays (modelling) of you and a co-facilitator having a conversation, or source a few video clips of people talking to each other, being relevant and not relevant. You could use the relevance clips on the *Talkabout* DVD as an alternative to the modelling.

Instructions

- Explain to the group that they are going to watch the facilitators have a conversation. In the first scenario, one facilitator asks a few questions and each time the other person answers in an irrelevant manner. Ask the group what they noticed. Was there anything not good? They will say you didn't answer the question (which was the previous topic) and you will introduce the word 'relevant' to them (if it has not already been mentioned).

- In the next role play, one facilitator asks the other a question such as 'What did you do at the weekend?' and the other person answers the question appropriately but then talks too much about a topic which they are clearly interested in. However, they go on about it and do not pick up the signs that the other person is obviously bored. Discuss with the group what the problem is with talking about our interests. Discuss the ways in which you can find out if the person is interested in a topic.

- In the next role play, ask the group to identify any signs that the second person may give to show you they are not interested. Repeat the previous role play but ask the group members to note all the little signs which show that they are not interested. For example: looking away, not responding much verbally or non-verbally, not asking any questions or commenting, fidgeting, and turning their legs or body away from the person speaking. Discuss the ways in which we can check if someone is interested and change the topic if not.

- In the next role play, ask the group to help you out. As you go through the role play, stop and ask for help. For example:

    F1: Did you have a nice weekend?

    F2: Yes thank you – I went to a dinosaur museum. Are you interested in dinosaurs?

    F1: Not really – sorry. But did you have a good day?

TALKABOUT Conversations ... Being relevant

Pause – ask the group what they think you should do now. How much can we say about the day at the dinosaur museum? One or two facts? What should we do then? Ask the group to help you decide how to change the topic.

- Continue with the group helping you to have a conversation which includes relevant topics that are interesting to both facilitators.

- Then the group can complete their worksheets. You could also refer to the worksheet in Activity 7 in the Body Language section for ideas on what people may think or feel if we are irrelevant.

- Distribute the handout and discuss the rules for being relevant.

Note on 'Learning to ...': now consider if any of the group members need to complete a 'Learning to ...' worksheet on relevance (a plan of action). If appropriate, refer to Activity 11 'Learning to look' in the Body Language section for instructions and the worksheet.

TALKABOUT Conversations ... Being relevant

Activity 16 'The rules for relevance' worksheet 1

Name .... Date ....

Poor relevance

❶ Talking about something that is not relevant ...

This means we may not answer someone's question or we talk about something that is not relevant to the person or to the situation.

If we talk about something that is not relevant:

The other person may think ....

The other person may feel ....

❷ Talking about something that is not interesting to the other person ...

This means we may talk about a subject that is not interesting to the other person. We may want to talk about it, but the other person is not interested.

If one person talks about something that is not interesting:

The other person may think ....

The other person may feel ....

TALKABOUT Conversations ... Being relevant

Activity 16 'The rules for relevance' worksheet 2

Name .... Date ....

I need to change the topic!

Signs to look out for ...

1 Their face ...

2 Their body ...

3 Their responses ...

ooh... interesting!

TALKABOUT Conversations ... Being relevant

Activity 16 'The rules for relevance' handout

Name .... Date ....

Relevance

What does being relevant mean?

 ✓ We need to talk about topics that are appropriate to the person and the situation

 ✓ We need to listen to the other person and answer their questions appropriately

 ✓ We need to make sure that the person is interested in what we are talking about

Why is this important?

It is important to be relevant in a conversation so that people want to talk to us. If we talk about things that are not relevant, other people may think we are rude and may not want to spend time with us any more.

TALKABOUT Conversations ... Being relevant

Activity 17 Dotty about ... dinosaurs

Preparation

Photocopy the worksheet.

Instructions

- This activity is only suitable for people who are focused on a few topics and struggle to expand what they talk about.

- Ask the group to brainstorm the topics of conversations they enjoy.

- Ask them to note how we are all different. You could ask everyone to identify those topics that have been mentioned that they would be interested in talking about and those that they are not so interested in.

- You may ask for someone to volunteer to talk about their main interest, eg dinosaurs. Complete the worksheet as a group activity and get help from those people who are not so interested in this topic. Consider ways they could change the topic and other topics they could talk about.

- Consider if it would help to have a time in the day when they are able to talk to someone about dinosaurs.

- Repeat this activity with other group members and their topics.

Variation

This activity could also be done individually.

TALKABOUT Conversations ... Being relevant

Activity 17 'Dotty about ... dinosaurs' worksheet

Name .... Date ....

I am very interested in ....

> What do I like about it?

> What do I like to talk to people about? Or ask people?

> If someone is not interested in this, what else could I talk about?

> What else might help me?

TALKABOUT Conversations ... Being relevant

Activity 18 Relevance time ... 'Linking words' and more

Additional activities for relevance

- **Linking words.** This is a good group cohesion activity when working on relevance. The first person thinks of a word and the next person says a word that is associated with it in some way. Continue this several times around the circle. You may like to ask people about their associations if some of them are not immediately apparent.

- **Change the topic.** Divide the group into smaller groups of two to four people. Prepare a few topics beforehand, eg food, school, television and film, hobbies, animals. One of the groups goes first and they are given two topics to talk about in a defined space of time (approximately 1–2 minutes). Ask them to talk about one topic and then move on to the next as smoothly as possible. The other group members observe and praise them for relevance and how easily they managed to change the topic.

- **Build a story.** One person starts a story by saying 'Once upon a time ...' Each group member then adds a sentence to create a story. One of the group facilitators can write down the story and read it back at the end. You can choose a theme for the story and/or have props in a bag to help people to bring in different ideas. For example, a bag with the following objects: a map, a teddybear, a purse, a pair of sunglasses and a photo of a man. Each person chooses an object and has to bring it into the story.

- **Relevant Robyn.** Ask the group to brainstorm a few scenarios such as meeting someone at a party; or making friends with someone at work; or talking to your grandparents, etc. Now think about what topics could be good to talk about. Divide the group into pairs and ask them to come up with a short role play showing good relevance. Each pair must decide who they are and what the conversation will be about and practise using good relevance. Make sure that everyone is comfortable taking part and check all role plays before the pairs perform them to the group.

TALKABOUT Conversations ... Repairing

Topic 7 Repairing

Activity 19 The rules for repairing

Preparation

You may need large sheets of paper and pens to write down the group discussion ideas.

Photocopy the worksheet and the handout.

You may want to prepare short role plays (modelling) of you and a co-facilitator having a conversation with inappropriate and appropriate repairing, or you could use the repairing clips on the Talkabout DVD as an alternative to the modelling.

Instructions

- Explain to the group that they are going to watch the facilitators have a conversation. In the first role play, use the scenario of meeting someone for the first time but one facilitator will mishear something. For example, the two facilitators could greet and introduce themselves but one mishears the other's name, eg Brandon instead of Brian. They then continue to call them by the wrong name for the rest of the conversation, maybe even entering the wrong name into their phone or on a form or sheet (so there is a consequence). The other facilitator continues to talk and does not correct the mistake. Other good things to show being misheard are: where someone lives, where you are meeting next week or someone's phone number.

- Ask the group what they noticed. Was there anything not good? They may say 'Yes' because you got their name wrong and then you could ask 'Why did I?' or 'Why did I keep getting it wrong?' If they haven't done so already, suggest that you will correct them and repair in the next role play.

- You can then do appropriate repairing in the next role play, keeping the situation and everything else the same as before.

- You may choose to do a third role play showing someone misunderstanding something in a conversation. This is more complicated, so only move on to this if you think the group will understand it. You need to think of a scenario where one facilitator is telling a story or explaining something and the other misunderstands or misinterprets it. It needs to be something quite obvious so that the group can see it. You could try something similar to the following scenario.

TALKABOUT Conversations ... Repairing

F1: Hi Beth, did you have a good weekend?

F2: Hi, well actually it wasn't great. I had an argument with my boyfriend.

F1: Oh no, that's horrible. What about?

F2: Oh just something little, it was nothing really but went on for a while!

F1: That sounds awful, it sounds like you two are going to break up, and after eight years! Don't worry, you will be fine and don't worry about that dinner party I'm having next week – you know the one on Thursday night?

F2: Yeah, I remember.

F1: Well no need to worry – he's no longer invited. In fact, I'm going to phone my friend Casper, you know the single one, and I'm going to get him to come instead. You would be great together! I'm going to set you up!

F2: Er, okay, um, can I give you a ring next week and let you know?

F1: No need, it's all sorted!

- Stop and ask the group if anything went wrong. They will say the second facilitator didn't want a new boyfriend, or she didn't break up with her boyfriend, or they may say the first facilitator overreacted. In that instance, you could then ask 'Why did they?', 'What did she think had happened?' and introduce the idea that the first facilitator had misunderstood the situation and then acted inappropriately because the second facilitator didn't correct and repair the mistake. Talk about the fact that there are consequences if we don't repair and make sure that people understand us correctly.

- You can then do the role play again with the same scenario but this time the second facilitator repairs and explains that she made up with her boyfriend and everything is OK.

- The group can then complete their worksheet, thinking of what other people may do or what might happen if we don't repair in a conversation.

- Then distribute the handout and discuss what it says and what we need to remember when repairing in a conversation.

TALKABOUT Conversations ... Repairing

Activity 19 'The rules for repairing' worksheet

Name .... Date ....

Poor repairing

❶ Someone has misheard us and we don't repair ...

This means the person we are talking to mishears something we have said, such as our name or where we live, and we don't correct them.

If we don't correct someone when they mishear us, what may happen?

....

....

❷ Someone has misunderstood us and we don't repair ...

This means the person we are talking to misunderstands what we have said or how we felt about a situation.

If we don't correct someone when they misunderstand us, what may happen?

....

....

Activity 19 'The rules for repairing' handout

Name .... Date ....

Repairing

What does repairing mean?

- ✓ Sometimes in a conversation the other person may mishear or misunderstand us

- ✓ We need to correct them otherwise they may go on to say or do something inappropriate

- ✓ We need to try to repair it as soon as possible

- ✓ We should politely say something like 'No, sorry, I meant ...' or 'No, it's Amy'

Why is this important?

It is important to repair in a conversation so that people understand us and what we have said. Repairing also means we keep the conversation relevant and flowing well. If we don't repair, people might not get to know us properly and conversations can get confusing.

TALKABOUT Conversations ... Repairing

Activity 20 Repairing time

Preparation

You will need a large sheet of paper and different coloured pens ready to write down the group's ideas.

Instructions

- Explain to the group that you are going to be thinking about repairing again today and all the times when people might misunderstand us.

- As a group, think of all the times when you have been misunderstood by someone who you are talking to. Write them all on the sheet.

- Next, get two different coloured pens and ask the group to circle with one colour all of the situations you have listed where someone has misheard you and, with the other colour, all of the situations where someone has misunderstood you. You could refer back to the worksheet from Activity 19 to remind you of the differences if needed.

- Now ask the group if they can think of any other situations or information that someone may mishear or misunderstand. Add these to the sheet and colour code them.

- Divide the group into pairs and get each pair to choose a different situation from your sheet of paper. As a pair, they must think about the situation and how you could appropriately repair to keep the conversation going and the information correct and relevant. They then create a short role play to show this. You may decide to all choose an easier scenario first where someone mishears them and then to do a second scenario where someone misunderstands them.

- Each pair performs their role play for the group and then the group discusses how they repaired in that situation and if that was appropriate.

TALKABOUT Conversations ... Ending a conversation

Topic 8 Ending a conversation

Activity 21 Listen to the ending

Preparation

You may need large sheets of paper and pens to write down the group discussion ideas.

Photocopy the worksheet.

You may want to prepare short role plays (modelling) of you and a co-facilitator ending a conversation, or source a few video clips of people ending conversations. You could use the 'Ending a conversation' clips on the Talkabout DVD as an alternative to the modelling.

Instructions

- Explain to the group that they are going to watch the facilitators have a conversation. Use a normal scenario such as what you did at the weekend. Have a good conversation, keeping everything appropriate and then, in the middle of one facilitator talking, the other one gets up and walks off. Ask the group what they noticed. Was there anything not good? They will say that you didn't say goodbye or you were rude and walked out. Ask the group what you should have done and they will say that you need to say goodbye. That facilitator says they will do better the next time and will say goodbye.

- In the next role play, use the same scenario of talking about your weekend. Have a good conversation and then, in the middle of one facilitator talking, the other says 'Goodbye' and walks off. Ask the group if that was better and they will say 'no' because you interrupted that person. Talk to the group about when it is OK to say goodbye and when it is not. Suggest that you need to wait for a pause or the end of a story before you say goodbye.

- In the third role play, keep the scenario the same and have an appropriate conversation about your weekend but, this time, the group facilitator waits for a natural pause or end of topic and then says goodbye very abruptly and walks off. Stop and ask the group if you did well this time. They will say 'no' because you left quickly and seemed rude. Discuss how you may give clues about wanting the conversation to end; what you may say so that the ending is not so sudden.

TALKABOUT Conversations ... Ending a conversation

Instructions (continued)

- In the next role play, the group facilitators have the same conversation about their weekend. This time, one of them waits for a natural pause, says a few phrases about needing to go as it is getting late, and says goodbye appropriately, but then uses inappropriate body language, for example kisses the co-facilitator (or attempts to) or gives them a hug, making them embarrassed or uncomfortable. Stop and ask the group if that was better. They will say 'no' because of the inappropriate body language.

  Discuss the fact that we need to get our non-verbal communication right and also use this to give clues that we want the conversation to end and then say goodbye appropriately too. Ask the group to give you suggestions for how you can use your body to show that you want to leave, eg look away, look bored, fidget or play with your keys.

- In the final role play, use the same scenario and then say goodbye appropriately, both verbally and non-verbally.

- After each role play, ask the group how it made the people appear.

- The group can then complete their worksheet. Also refer to Activity 7 in the Body Language section if needed. Add to the ideas you have come up with throughout the role plays of how you can show you want to end a conversation.

TALKABOUT Conversations ... Ending a conversation

Activity 21 'Listen to the ending' worksheet

Name .... Date ....

Poor endings

❶ Poor endings ...

This means we say the wrong things when ending a conversation or we don't use our bodies to show we want to finish. We may use an inappropriate touch to end with or we may not do or say anything and just walk off.

If we don't end a conversation appropriately:

The other person may think ....

The other person may feel ....

❷ How can we show that we want to end a conversation?

....

....

....

TALKABOUT Conversations ... Ending a conversation

Activity 22 The rules for ending a conversation

Preparation

Photocopy the worksheet. Enlarge them to A3 size if you are completing this activity as a group activity.

Photocopy the handout.

Instructions

- Explain to the group that in a conversation it is not always you who wants it to finish. Sometimes the other person wants the conversation to finish because they need to leave or have said what they wanted to. Therefore, we also need to look at their body language and their non-verbal cues. We need to look for clues that they would like the conversation to end.

- Begin by asking the group what they think you may see someone doing if they want to end a conversation. Write down any ideas. Then get the worksheet out and talk about how there are three main areas we need to look at for clues: their face, their body and their responses. Explain what we mean by each of these.

- Complete the worksheet as a group, collating everyone's ideas, or split the group into pairs to fill in the sheet and then all return and give feedback. The main answers you are hoping for are:

    o **their face** – facial expression looks bored, eye contact lessens and they may look away, or at the door, or at their watch

    o **their body** – they may turn their body away, or their feet may point towards the door, or they may fidget, pack up or look for their keys

    o **their responses** – they will talk less or just make noises, they will stop asking questions or only ask closed questions, they may say things such as 'right' or 'okay' or even 'Wow it's late, I should be going'.

Note on 'Learning to ...': now consider whether any of the group members need to complete a 'Learning to ...' worksheet on ending a conversation (a plan of action). If appropriate, refer to Activity 11 'Learning to look' in the Body Language section for instructions and the worksheet.

TALKABOUT Conversations ... Ending a conversation

Activity 22 'The rules for ending a conversation' worksheet

Name .... Date ....

I need to end the conversation!

Signs to look out for ...

❶ Their face ...

❷ Their body ...

❸ Their responses ...

TALKABOUT Conversations ... Ending a conversation

Activity 22 'The rules for ending a conversation' handout

Name ……………………………………………………….. Date …………………….

Ending conversations

What does a good ending mean?

 ✓ If we need to end a conversation, we should start to talk less and not ask any questions

 ✓ We need to wait for a pause in the conversation or the end of a topic or story

 ✓ We may give some non-verbal signs we want to end such as fidgeting or looking away

 ✓ We can then say goodbye appropriately, use touch if appropriate and then leave

❗ Why is this important?

It is polite to end a conversation appropriately and then people are more likely to want to talk to us again. We must use our verbal and non-verbal skills so that we appear polite and friendly.

If we don't end a conversation appropriately, people may think we don't like talking to them or that we are not interested.

TALKABOUT Conversations ... Ending a conversation

Activity 23 Conversation critic

Preparation

Source some clips of people having conversations from some of the group members' favourite television programmes or films.

Photocopy the worksheet, either one per pair or one enlarged to A3 size if you are working as a group.

Instructions

- Explain to the group that you are going to be analysing the endings of conversations today. You are also going to be thinking about all of the things you have learned about conversations over the past weeks.

- Divide the group into pairs and give each pair a worksheet. Alternatively, work as one big group with a larger worksheet in the middle. Go through the worksheet together, explaining that you want them to watch the conversation and think about three parts.

    The beginning: how did the conversation start and was this appropriate? **The middle**: did the conversation flow well? Did they take turns and ask and answer questions appropriately? And then **the ending**: how did the conversation end? Was this appropriate? Remind the group that they need to consider whether the conversational parts were appropriate for the setting and also the people involved.

- Choose the first video clip and show it to the group. On first viewing, tell the group not to write down anything, just watch and listen. When it has finished, ask them what they noticed, good and bad, and add this to the worksheet.

- Then play the video clip again so that the group can note down anything else they have missed. If working in pairs, each pair then shares their ideas and observations. The group decides whether it was a good or bad conversation and if anything could have been improved.

- Repeat the activity with another conversation clip.

TALKABOUT Conversations ... Ending a conversation

Activity 23 'Conversation critic' worksheet

Name .... Date ....

What was the setting?

How did the conversation start? Was it appropriate?

How did they keep the conversation going?
(Did they take turns, ask and answer questions, repair and keep relevant?)

How did the conversation end? Was it appropriate?

Is there anything they could have improved?

TALKABOUT Conversations ... Ending a conversation

Activity 24 Ending time ... 'Ending Eddie' and more

Additional activities for ending a conversation

- **Ending Eddie.** Print or draw several blank speech bubbles. As a group, think of all the things you could say to end a conversation. Think about things you have used before and new ideas the group have had. Write each idea on a speech bubble. Then divide the group into pairs and give them each a simple scenario, such as having dinner with a friend, talking to the dentist, asking for information at the library, etc. Each pair decides who they will be in the scenario and creates a short relevant conversation. They can look at all of the possible ways to end a conversation and decide which would work best in their scenario. The pairs then perform their role plays to the group and the group discusses whether the ending was appropriate for the scenario.

- **Tell me a story.** This is similar to the story activity in Activity 23. One person starts a story by saying 'Once upon a time ...' Going round the group clockwise, each group member then adds a sentence to create a story. After one round, the person sitting to the right of the group member who started has to end the story in some way. One of the group facilitators can write down the story and then read it back at the end. You can choose a theme for the story and/or have props in a bag to help people to bring in different ideas. Once you have played one round, the next group member starts a story with the person to their right ending it. Continue until everyone has had a chance to start and end the story. Discuss how it went and the difficulties in finishing the story if it was in the middle of something happening. Think about how this is similar to a conversation.

TALKABOUT Conversations... How did I do?

Topic 9 How did I do?

Activity 25 Conversational skills ... what am I like? (part 2)

Preparation

Photocopy new assessment sheets. Make sure that you have the completed assessment sheets and target sheets from Activity 3, one for each group member.

Photocopy the certificate of achievement.

Instructions

- Ask the group to consider how they have got on over the last few weeks and whether they think they have improved.

- As a group, go through the 'What am I like?' assessment sheet and ask where they would rate themselves now.

- Then ask the group members to think individually about where they are with their conversational skills now and to mark this on their sheet. They may want to sit in different parts of the room to be more private.

- The group facilitator(s) then discusses with each group member how they have rated themselves and compare this with their original assessment sheet.

- The group members are then given a certificate of achievement.

TALKABOUT Conversations... How did I do?

Activity 25 'What am I like? (part 2)' assessment sheet

Name .... Date ....

Conversational skills ... what am I like?

	Never good	Not very good	Quite good	Very good
❶ Listening				
❷ Starting a conversation				
❸ Taking turns				
❹ Asking questions				
❺ Answering questions				
❻ Being relevant				
❼ Repairing				
❽ Ending a conversation				

TALKABOUT Conversations … How did I do?

Certificate of Achievement

THIS IS TO CERTIFY THAT

....

HAS COMPLETED TALKABOUT LEVEL 3

CONVERSATIONAL SKILLS

SIGNED .... DATE ....

Level 4 Talkabout Assertiveness

Introduction

Objectives To introduce the difference between being passive, aggressive and assertive.

To introduce the eight assertiveness skills:
- expressing feelings
- standing up for yourself
- making suggestions
- refusing
- disagreeing
- complaining
- apologising
- requesting explanations.

Materials You will need to photocopy several of the activities.

Some of the activity worksheets are best enlarged to A3 size.

Some of the activity cards are best laminated so that you can use them again.

Some activities are designed to be A5 to create a 'fact book' for social skills.

Timing The topics in Level 4 will take up to 35 sessions to complete.

TALKABOUT Assertiveness

Contents — page

Topic 1 Talkabout assertiveness

Activity 1	What is assertiveness?	238
Activity 2	What does assertiveness look like?	243
Activity 3	Being passive	249
Activity 4	Being aggressive	251
Activity 5	Being assertive	253
Activity 6	Assertiveness … what am I like? (part 1)	257

Topic 2 Expressing feelings

Activity 7	Emotions recap	260
Activity 8	What could I do?	261
Activity 9	The rules for expressing feelings	264
Activity 10	My STAR plan for expressing feelings	266
Activity 11	Express yourself	268

Topic 3 Standing up for yourself

Activity 12	Standing tall	269
Activity 13	The rules for standing up for yourself	271
Activity 14	Stand by Houston!	273

Topic 4 Making suggestions

Activity 15	The negotiating game	274
Activity 16	The rules for making suggestions	277
Activity 17	Suggestion time	279

Topic 5 Refusing

Activity 18	Saying 'no'	280
Activity 19	The rules for refusing	286
Activity 20	The refusing game	288

TALKABOUT Assertiveness

Topic 6 Disagreeing

Activity 21	The disagreeing game	289
Activity 22	Why is disagreeing important?	293
Activity 23	The rules for disagreeing	295
Activity 24	Disagree dilemma	297

Topic 7 Complaining

Activity 25	Complaining time	298
Activity 26	The rules for complaining	301
Activity 27	The complaining game	302

Topic 8 Apologising

Activity 28	Saying sorry	303
Activity 29	The sorry scale	305
Activity 30	The rules for apologising	309
Activity 31	The apologising game	311

Topic 9 Requesting explanations

Activity 32	Requesting time	312
Activity 33	The rules for requesting explanations	314
Activity 34	The requesting game	316

Topic 10 My assertiveness

Activity 35	Assertiveness … what am I like? (part 2)	317

TALKABOUT Assertiveness

Topic 1 Talkabout assertiveness

Activity 1 What is assertiveness?

Preparation

Photocopy and cut out the scenario cards. Laminate them if you want to use them again.

Photocopy the assertive scale. You could enlarge it to A3 size and laminate it if you wish to use it again.

Instructions

- Explain to the group that you are going to be starting a new topic today. Place the assertive scale in the middle of the group and the pile of scenario cards face-down beside it.

- Ask the group to take it in turns to pick up a card and read out the scenario. They decide whether the story shows someone being passive, aggressive or assertive and place it on the scale accordingly. The group can help give ideas if the group member is struggling.

- The next person then takes a card and repeats the process. Continue until all of the cards have been read, discussed and placed on the scale.

- Summarise the activity by beginning to discuss what common traits we are seeing in the passive, aggressive or assertive card scenarios.

Note: you may like to take a photograph or note down where each card is placed because in later activities you will be recommended to refer back to each area and its scenarios.

Variation

You could prepare short role plays (modelling) to introduce this topic. Use a simple scenario such as your co-facilitator asking you to change your plans so that they can come round for dinner because they are on their own tonight. You will need to prepare three role plays: one where you respond passively (try to explain you have plans but then agree to cancel them); one where you respond aggressively (don't listen to the request and not even consider changing your plans); and a final one in which you respond assertively (inviting her to join your plans). After each role play, ask the group what they noticed and what you should do differently.

Alternatively, you could watch and discuss the assertiveness clips on the Talkabout DVD.

TALKABOUT Assertiveness

Activity 1 'What is assertiveness?' scenario cards

✂

Amy is very cross with Raj because he has forgotten her birthday. She shouts at him in front of their friends.

Hayley is fed up. Her boss has asked her to stay late and finish an important job. Hayley says 'No way' and then swears at her boss and storms off home.

Rebecca is cross. She is supposed to be meeting Nevin for coffee but Nevin is late. Rebecca phones another friend and sends Nevin a rude text telling her not to bother coming.

Chris is furious. He has just bought a game from a shop but it doesn't work. He rushes back to the shop and shouts at the shop assistant and demands another one.

Ed is talking to Tanvi who is not very happy at work. Ed doesn't listen to what Tanvi is saying and tells her she is being silly and to just look for another job.

Grace is worried. She has been asked to do a job at work which she doesn't understand. She decides not to say anything and hope for the best.

TALKABOUT Assertiveness

Activity 1 'What is assertiveness?' scenario cards

Mohammed is upset. Someone at work has been saying mean things about him. He doesn't want to make a fuss, so says nothing.

Joley is feeling ill and knows she should go to see her doctor. She is worried that the doctor will be cross with her for wasting his time, so she decides to wait and see if she feels better soon.

Tomas is upset. Someone at work keeps taking his packed lunch and eating it. Tomas decides to eat everyone's lunch and see how they like it!

Zara is talking to her friend Sophie. Sophie is trying to persuade Zara to go out with her this weekend but Zara is supposed to be helping her mum. Zara is finding it difficult to say 'no'.

Lisa is getting cross. She has been working hard today and wants to leave work on time. Her work mates are messing about, not doing their jobs. Lisa suggests that they all work together and try to leave on time.

Vincent is worried. He teased Helen this morning and he knows it has upset her. He decides to talk to Helen immediately and say sorry.

TALKABOUT Assertiveness

Activity 1 'What is assertiveness?' scenario cards

✂

Rachel is feeling upset. Her friend Sue has made fun of her in front of some other people. Rachel decides to tell Sue that she is hurt by what she said.	**Jo** is worried. Her friends are deciding what to do. Someone suggests going round to Ferhan's house and surprising him. Jo knows Ferhan would hate this as he is studying, so Jo disagrees and tells them why.
Marnie is cross. Her boss has asked her to work at the weekend but Marnie is going to a wedding. She goes to see her boss and says she can't work this weekend and explains why	**Naomi** is confused. Her boss has left her a note asking her to do a job but she doesn't understand what she means. Naomi arranges to go and talk to her boss and ask her to explain.
Emily is upset. She has been telling everyone how she is now a vegetarian. Adam was mean and made fun of her. Emily decides to stand up for herself and tells Adam why being a vegetarian can be good.	**Anya** is annoyed. She ordered her food ages ago and now it has arrived and is wrong. She asks to talk to the manager and explains that she is not happy.

TALKABOUT Assertiveness

Assertiveness scale

Passive — Assertive — Aggressive

1....2....3....4....5....6....7....8....9....10

TALKABOUT Assertiveness

Activity 2 What does assertiveness look like?

Preparation

Photocopy the three worksheets, which you may like to enlarge to A3 size.

Photocopy the cards; enlarge the sheet to A3 first if you have enlarged the three worksheets. You will also need scissors and glue.

Instructions

- Place the three worksheets in the middle of the group. Explain that they are going to continue their work on assertiveness. You could use the scale from Activity 1 and recap on the basic descriptions for each word you came up with in the previous session.

- Cut out all of the cards. Mix them up and get each group member in turn to read one out and decide whether it describes a passive person, an assertive person or an aggressive person. Sort all of the cards and stick them on the three worksheets.

- Next, look at the three 'consequence' labels. Read out each one in turn and as a group decide which worksheet it belongs to.

- Once you have completed each worksheet, read through them one at a time and discuss what is meant by passive, aggressive and assertive. Which do the group think is the best way to act? Does anyone think they are more passive or aggressive at times?

- You may like to photocopy the finished worksheets so that each individual can have a copy.

Variation

This activity could be done as a worksheet activity where the group members cut out and stick the descriptors (the cards) on their individual worksheets.

TALKABOUT Assertiveness

Activity 2 'What does assertiveness look like?' cards

Think before they speak

Rude to people

Good listener

Talks to people

Shouts

Looks away

Good eye contact

Stares

Worries about talking to people

Interrupts a lot

Quiet, mumbling voice

Doesn't listen

TALKABOUT Assertiveness

Activity 2 'What does assertiveness look like?' cards

No gestures

No words come out

Voice is clear

Upright posture

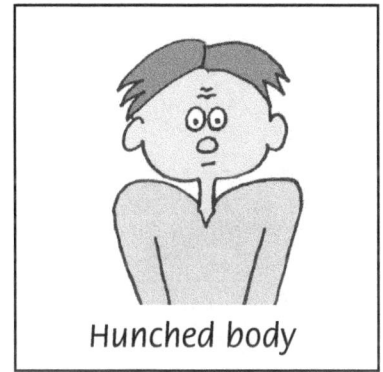
Hunched body

Angry gestures

Consequence labels

They do not respond to hurtful situations. They allow problems to continue. They may have an outburst when they can't take any more. They often feel guilty and confused.

They respect others' opinions and listen respectfully. They realise it is important to speak honestly and are confident about who they are. They address issues and take responsibility for their own happiness.

They dominate and control people by either being rude or manipulating a situation. They criticise and blame others. They become isolated from people and not many like them.

TALKABOUT Assertiveness

Activity 2 'What does assertiveness look like?' worksheet 1

Name .... Date ....

A passive person ... what do you see?

Passive ...

Speech bubbles: "I lose, you win" — "er..." — "Sorry, sorry, sorry..."

TALKABOUT Assertiveness

Activity 2 'What does assertiveness look like?' worksheet 2

Name .... Date ....

An aggressive person ... what do you see?

"I win, you lose ..."

"That's your problem"

Aggressive ...

?

TALKABOUT Assertiveness

Activity 2 'What does assertiveness look like?' worksheet 3

Name .... Date ....

An assertive person ... what do you see?

I win, you win

I believe...

Assertive ...

?

TALKABOUT Assertiveness

Activity 3 Being passive

Preparation

Photocopy the worksheet. You may like to enlarge it to A3 size.

You will also need a marker pen.

Instructions

- Explain to the group that you are going to think about being passive. You could use the scale from Activity 1 and the summary sheet from Activity 2 to remind the group what this means, or watch the passive clip from the Talkabout DVD (scene 32).

- Get the group to think about times when they have been passive. This could be at home, with friends, at school, college or work, etc. Try to come up with at least four situations as a group when people have been passive and add them to the worksheet.

- When a few situations have been written down, ask the group to think about what happened in each case and what could have been done to appear more assertive. Add these ideas to the worksheet.

- Discuss as a group how we can all be passive at times but we need to know how we can be more assertive when we need to express something and get our ideas or opinions across.

Variation
The group members could first think about situations when they have been passive, either on their own or in pairs, before feeding their ideas back to the group.

TALKABOUT Assertiveness

Activity 3 'Being passive' worksheet

How could I have been more assertive?

TALKABOUT Assertiveness

Activity 4 Being aggressive

Preparation

Photocopy the worksheet. You may like to enlarge it to A3 size.

You will also need a marker pen.

Instructions

- Explain to the group that today you are going to think about being aggressive. You could use the scale from Activity 1 and summary sheet from Activity 2 to remind the group what this means, or watch the aggressive clip from the Talkabout DVD (scene 32).

- Ask the group to think about times when they have been aggressive. This could be at home, with friends, at school, college or work, etc. Try to come up with at least four situations as a group when people have been aggressive and add them to the worksheet.

- When a few situations have been written down, ask the group to think about what happened in each case and what could have been done to appear more assertive. Add these ideas to the sheet.

- Discuss as a group how we can all feel angry or annoyed at times but we need to know how we can be assertive to express ideas or opinions in an appropriate and effective way.

Variation
The group members could think first about situations when they have been aggressive, either on their own or in pairs, before feeding their ideas back to the group.

Activity 4 'Being aggressive' worksheet

How could I have been more assertive?

TALKABOUT Assertiveness

Activity 5 Being assertive

Preparation

Photocopy the 'Assertiveness' board and the cards. Laminate the board and cards if you want to use them again. You could also stick a small piece of Velcro™ on the back of each card with a corresponding piece on each square of the board.

Photocopy the handout.

Instructions

- Collect together the scenarios from Activity 1 which the group rated as being assertive; there should be eight of them. Read them through together one-by-one and talk about what that person is doing.

- As the group members say each behaviour from the scenarios, discuss how this shows someone is being assertive and add it to the 'Assertiveness' board; for example, 'this person is expressing their feelings'.

- Continue until you have discussed all eight aspects and added them to the board. Summarise by talking about all of the different things we do to show that we are assertive.

- You can then give each group member the summary handout to add to their workbook if they are completing one.

Variation
Put all of the cards in a bag or in a pile face-down in the middle of the group. The group members take it in turns to pick a card and then tell the group how that behaviour shows you are assertive. The group then discusses whether everyone agrees.

TALKABOUT Assertiveness

Activity 5 'Being assertive' board

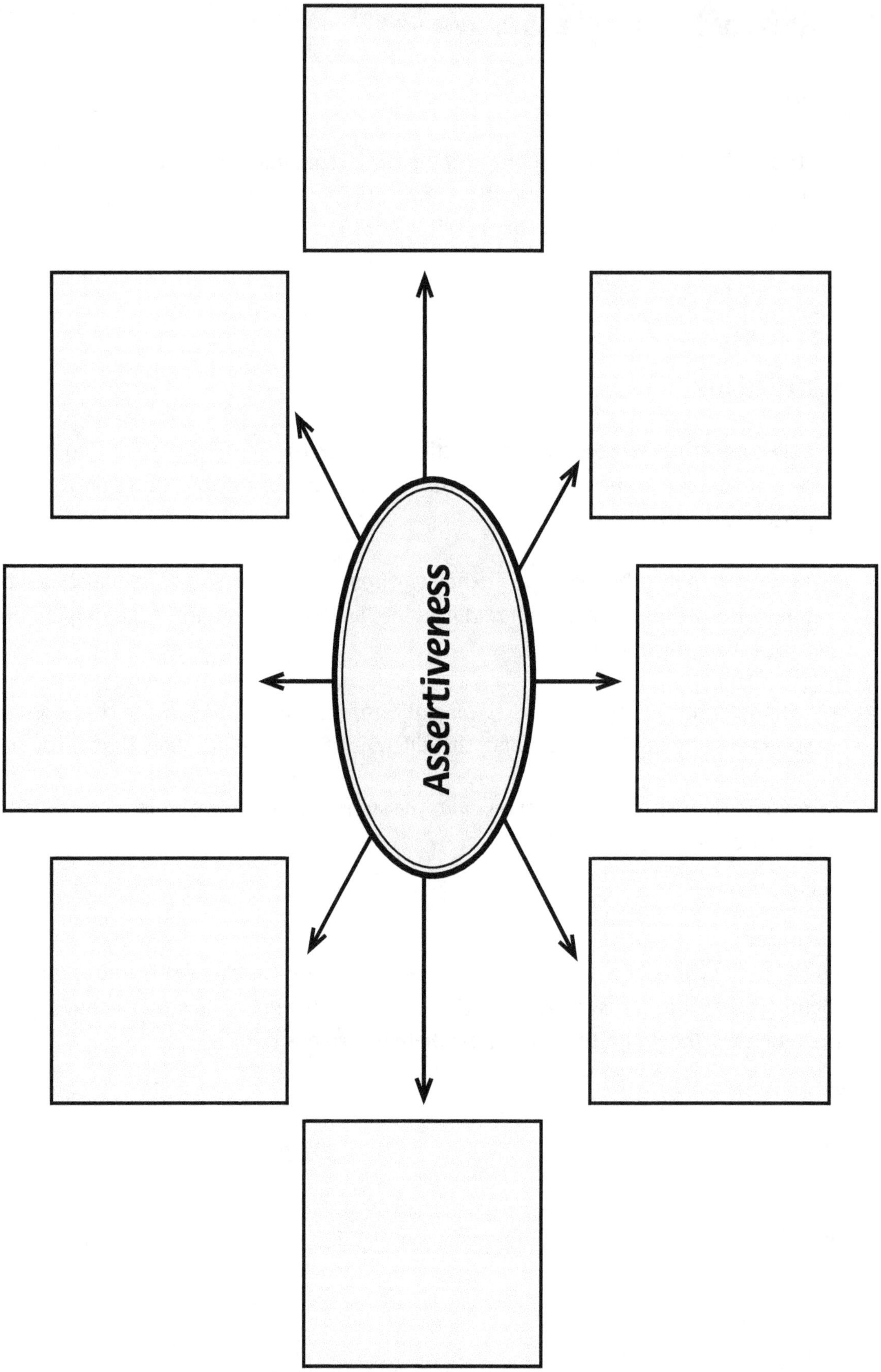

Assertiveness

TALKABOUT Assertiveness

Activity 5 'Being assertive' cards

expressing feelings

standing up for yourself

making suggestions

refusing

disagreeing

complaining

apologising

requesting explanations

TALKABOUT Assertiveness

Activity 5 'Being assertive' handout

Name .... Date ....

Being assertive means ...

- making suggestions ("Can I make a suggestion?")
- refusing ("No, I don't want to go...")
- disagreeing ("I disagree")
- requesting explanations ("I'd like to ask")
- apologising ("I'm sorry!")
- complaining ("This soup is cold")
- expressing feelings ("I feel...")
- standing up for yourself ("This is ME!")

256 This page may be photocopied for instructional use only. *Talkabout Second Edition* © Alex Kelly, 2016

TALKABOUT Assertiveness

Activity 6 Assertiveness ... what am I like? (part 1)

Preparation

Photocopy the assessment sheet, one for each group member. You may like to enlarge one to A3 size to use in group discussion.

Photocopy a target sheet for each group member.

Instructions

- Remind the group that they are going to be focusing on assertive skills for the next few sessions. Therefore, they are going to plan what they need to work on.

- As a group, go through the 'What am I like?' sheet, explaining the different behaviours and the rating scale. It is a good idea to get the group used to the rating scale first by rating everyday skills such as cooking, cycling, getting out of bed in the morning, etc.

- Then ask the group members to think individually about where they are with their assertive skills. They may want to sit in different parts of the room to be more private.

- The group facilitator then discusses with each group member how they have rated themselves. The facilitators then share how they rated that group member on their Talkabout assessment summary wheel (only the 'assertiveness' section), raising awareness of what they need to improve on and what they are already doing well.

- The group members can then complete a target sheet for the Assertiveness topic.

TALKABOUT Assertiveness

Activity 6 'Assertiveness ... what am I like?' assessment

Name .... Date ....

Assertiveness ... what am I like at it?

	Never good	Not very good	Quite good	Very good
1 Expressing feelings *(I feel...)*				
2 Standing up for yourself *(This is ME!)*				
3 Making Suggestions *(I suggest..)*				
4 Refusing *(NO!)*				
5 Disagreeing *(I disagree...)*				
6 Complaining *(This soup is cold)*				
7 Apologising *(I'm sorry!)*				
8 Requesting explanations *(I'd like to ask)*				

TALKABOUT Assertiveness

Activity 6 'Assertiveness … what am I like?' target sheet

Name ……………………………………………………….. Date ………………………

My Assertiveness plan

 **I am good at …**

I need to work on …

How did I get on?

TALKABOUT Assertiveness ... Expressing feelings

Topic 2 Expressing feelings

Activity 7 Emotions recap

Preparation

Photocopy and cut out the feeling cards from Level 1 Body Language, Activity 15 'Different feelings'. These are best laminated if you want to use them again.

Create two more cards with the headings 'Difficult to talk about' and 'Easy to talk about'. You may want to laminate them if you would like to use them again.

You will also need a large sheet of paper and pens.

Instructions

- Begin this topic by recapping on how we express different feelings. Place the two heading cards on the table or on the floor in the middle of the group. Explain to the group that they are going to be thinking about feelings and which ones are harder to express and which ones are easier.

- Place the feeling cards in a pile face-down and get each group member in turn to select a card, read it and then discuss as a group whether this feeling is easy or hard to express. The group members may also think of other feelings that are easy or difficult to express and these can be added.

- Once you have sorted all of the feelings into the two categories, talk about why some feelings are harder to express. What is it about them?

- Next, choose one of the feelings you have sorted as 'difficult to talk about' and brainstorm as a group all of the things that might make you feel that feeling, eg all of the things that make us angry. Write these on the large sheet of paper.

- If there is time, choose another one or two feelings and do the same.

- Keep your brainstorming sheet safe as you will need it for the next activity.

TALKABOUT Assertiveness ... Expressing feelings

Activity 8 What could I do?

Preparation

Photocopy the cards and the worksheet. You may like to enlarge them to A3 size.

You will also need scissors and glue.

Instructions

- Ask the group to consider one of the scenarios and feelings from Activity 7. Explain that they are going to decide what it would be best to do in that situation.

- Cut out all of the cards and take it in turns to consider them and decide whether they are OK or not OK (or 'good ideas' and 'bad ideas').

- Ask the group to look at the cards that have been considered OK. What might you do first? The group will probably choose the three cards that describe 'stopping'.

- Talk about the need to first 'Stop'. There are three cards that can summarise this and you can talk about the need to 'Stop for a minute', 'Walk away from the situation' and 'Count to ten, breathe and calm down'. These can then be placed or stuck in the three boxes on the worksheet.

- What would you do next? Second, talk about the need to 'Think'. There are three cards that can summarise this: 'Take some time to think', 'Think about what I should say' and 'Think about what I should do'.

- Third, we need to 'Act'. There are three cards that summarise this: 'Talk to someone', 'Tell someone how I feel' and 'Ask someone for help or their opinion'.

- These cards can be stuck on the worksheet either as part of the group activity or as individual worksheets.

TALKABOUT Assertiveness ... **Expressing feelings**

Activity 8 'What could I do?' cards

 Think about what I should say	 Stop for a minute	 Tell someone how I feel
 Talk to someone	 Shout lots	 Think about what I should do
 Walk away from the situation	 Do or say nothing	 Take some time to think
 Hit or throw something	 Count to ten, breathe and calm down	 Ask someone for help or their opinion

TALKABOUT Assertiveness ... Expressing feelings

Activity 8 'What could I do?' worksheet

Name .... Date ....

1 Stop

2 Think

3 Act

TALKABOUT Assertiveness ... Expressing feelings

Activity 9 The rules for expressing feelings

Preparation

Photocopy the handout. Cut them to size if the group members are going to put them in their A5 fact book.

You may want to prepare short role plays (modelling) of you and a co-facilitator having a conversation, or source a few video clips of people expressing their feelings in a conversation. You could use the 'Expressing Feelings' clip on the Talkabout DVD as an alternative to the modelling.

Instructions

- Explain to the group that they are going to watch the facilitators have a conversation. Use a simple scenario, for example, telling your co-facilitator that you are annoyed or sad because they are late, have broken something or have upset you.

- In the first role play, the group facilitator should express their feelings passively and maybe even blame themselves for getting the time wrong or moving the broken object. Ask the group what they noticed. Was there anything not good about it? They will say the group facilitator didn't speak strongly enough or say how they really felt.

- In the next role play, use the same scenario but, this time, the group facilitator expresses their feelings aggressively. They shout and use aggressive body language, and may not listen to the other facilitator. Ask the group if that was better, if you were stronger. They will say 'no' because you were mean or aggressive.

- In the third roleplay, express your feelings assertively.

- Ask the group to consider why it is important to say how you are feeling. Think about how it is best to do this assertively.

- Ask the group what happens if we don't do this? How do we appear?

- Distribute the handout and discuss the rules for expressing feelings.

TALKABOUT Assertiveness ... Expressing feelings

Activity 9 'The rules for expressing feelings' handout

Name .... Date ....

Expressing feelings

How should we express our feelings?

✓ Stop and think about what you are feeling and what you should do

✓ Remember to use good body language

✓ Use a calm voice and speak clearly

✓ Say how you feel and explain why you feel like that. Try saying 'I feel … because …'

Why is this important?

It is important to be able to express our feelings clearly and appropriately so that other people can understand how we are feeling. They may be able to help us feel better or help us to find a good solution to the problem. If we don't tell people how we feel, they may think we are rude or don't care. We may also feel worse if we don't tell someone how we are feeling.

Activity 10 My STAR plan for expressing feelings

Preparation

Photocopy the worksheet and enlarge it to A3 size if you are completing this activity as a group. Photocopy A4-sized copies if the group members are completing the sheet individually.

Note: this worksheet will also be used for future activities.

Instructions

- Ask the group to think of a few situations where they would like to express how they are feeling. The group could think about situations that have happened before but choose one that may arise again which they could plan for.

- Think about the STAR plan (Stop, Think, Act, Reflect). Can they decide what they should do in each area? They could refer back to the worksheet in Activity 8 for ideas. Which would work best for their situation?

- The group then completes a worksheet either together or individually if they have a specific situation that they would like to plan. They can then feed back their ideas to the group.

- If this is completed as a group, photocopy the worksheet to go in the group members' fact books if appropriate.

TALKABOUT Assertiveness ... Expressing feelings

Activity 10 'My STAR plan' worksheet

Name .... Date ....

My plan for ....

Describe the situation ...

Stop ... How do I feel?

Think ... What do I want to say or do? Who should I talk to?

Act ... What will I do? What will I say?

Reflect ... What will the consequence be? How will I feel?

You could now practise this through role play!

TALKABOUT Assertiveness ... Expressing feelings

Activity 11 Express yourself

Preparation

None needed.

Instructions

- Explain to the group that you are going to act out different scenarios and practise expressing feelings appropriately. Consider some of the scenarios that you have discussed in the previous activity.

- Divide the group into pairs and give each pair a scenario. Give them time to create a short role play around that situation.

- The pair must decide who they are in the scenario and then plan how they should express their feelings appropriately, thinking about the rules.

- The pairs then take it in turns to perform their role play to the group who could then comment on whether they expressed their feelings assertively.

- This activity is repeated as necessary until everyone feels confident. They may like to practise outside the group and feed back their successes and their difficulties in the next session.

TALKABOUT Assertiveness ... Standing up for yourself

Topic 3 Standing up for yourself

Activity 12 Standing tall

Preparation

You will need a large sheet of paper and a pen.

Photocopy the worksheet and enlarge it to A3 size.

You may want to prepare short role plays (modelling) of you and a co-facilitator having a conversation, or source a few video clips of people standing up for themselves in a conversation. You could use the 'Standing up for yourself' clip on the Talkabout DVD as an alternative to the modelling.

Instructions

- Explain to the group that they are going to watch the facilitators have a conversation. Use a simple scenario such as your co-facilitator teasing you about something you believe in or really like. In the first role play, the group facilitator should stand up for themselves passively and not even attempt to argue or express their opinions. Ask the group what they noticed. Was there anything not good about it? They will say the group facilitator didn't speak strongly enough or give their feelings or opinions.

- In the next role play, use the same scenario but, this time, the group facilitator stands up for themselves aggressively. They shout and use aggressive body language; they could criticise the co-facilitator's lack of belief or things they like. Ask the group if that was better and they will say 'no' because you were mean, aggressive or rude.

- In the third role play, stand up for yourself assertively.

- The group then discuss what they think standing up for yourself means and the things they need to remember when doing it to come across in an assertive way.

- Ask the group to think about all the times when they had to stand up for themselves or situations where they imagine they may have to do this. For example, if someone is making fun of the fact that they are a vegetarian. Write them all down on the large sheet of paper.

- Complete the worksheet as a group with everyone's ideas.

TALKABOUT Assertiveness ... Standing up for yourself

Activity 12 'Standing tall' worksheet

Name .... Date ....

Standing up for myself

? What does standing up for myself mean?

 What do I need to remember to do?

TALKABOUT Assertiveness ... Standing up for yourself

Activity 13 The rules for standing up for yourself

Preparation

Photocopy the handout. Cut them to size if the group members are going to put them in their A5 fact book.

Instructions

- Explain to the group that you are going to consider the rules for standing up for yourself appropriately and effectively.

- Ask the group to consider why it is important to stand up for yourself. Think about how it is best to do this assertively.

- What happens if we don't do this? How do we appear?

- Distribute the handout and discuss what it says.

Note on STAR plan: now complete a STAR plan for standing up for yourself. See Activity 10 for the instructions and worksheet.

TALKABOUT Assertiveness ... Standing up for yourself

Activity 13 'The rules for standing up for yourself' handout

Name .... Date ....

Standing up for yourself

How should we stand up for ourselves?

 ✓ Stop and think – do you agree with what is being said or done? What should you do?

 ✓ Remember to use assertive body language to show that you are confident in what you think

 ✓ Use a calm voice and speak clearly. Try saying 'I think … because …'

 Why is this important?

It is important to be able to stand up for ourselves clearly and appropriately, so that other people know what we think and feel. It will allow us to say what we believe in and give our opinions.

If we don't stand up for ourselves, other people won't know how we feel about something. They may think we are weak or boring.

TALKABOUT Assertiveness ... Standing up for yourself

Activity 14 Stand by Houston!

Preparation

None needed.

Instructions

- Explain to the group that you are going to act out different scenarios and practise standing up for yourself appropriately. Consider some of the scenarios that you have discussed in Activity 12.

- Divide the group into pairs and give each pair a scenario. Give them time to create a short role play around that situation.

- The pair must decide who they are in the scenario and then plan how they should stand up for themselves appropriately, thinking about the rules.

- The pairs then take it in turns to perform their role play to the group who could then comment on whether they stood up for themselves assertively.

- Repeat this activity as necessary until everyone feels confident. They may like to practise outside the group and feed back their successes and their difficulties in the next session.

TALKABOUT Assertiveness ... Making suggestions

Topic 4 Making suggestions

Activity 15 The negotiating game

Preparation

Photocopy the topic cards. Laminate them if you want to use them again.

Photocopy the worksheet and enlarge it to A3 size.

Instructions

- Sitting in a circle, explain to the group that you are going to have a discussion. It would be good for everyone to be part of the discussion and to share at least one thing if they can.

- Choose a topic card and read it to the group. The group then discusses this, considering all options. Let the discussion continue for a few minutes, or until a plan or decision has been reached and agreed by the group (or the majority of it).

- When the discussion has ended, ask the group how it went. Which suggestions did they listen to and why? How did people respond to the suggestions? Did everyone make a suggestion and, if not, why?

- You could then choose another topic and have a second discussion, asking the group members to think about the suggestions and how they were made.

- The group can then complete the worksheet to summarise their ideas from the activity about making suggestions. Think about how we make suggestions. Also add some ideas about how we can begin a suggestion, eg 'I think we should ...', 'Maybe you could ...', 'Why don't we ...?', etc.

Variation

Split the group into two smaller groups. Give one group a scenario to discuss while the other group observes and then, at the end, gives feedback. Change over so that both groups get a chance to observe.

You could also watch the 'Making suggestions' clip on the Talkabout DVD for ideas.

TALKABOUT Assertiveness ... Making suggestions

Activity 15 'The negotiating game' topic cards

Decide on a meal which the group members should all have for dinner.	The group has been given some money. What should it be spent on?
The group has permission to go on a trip next week. Where should you go?	Decide on a film the group members could all watch in the next session.
There are two tickets to the theatre tonight. Who in the group should go?	Someone has brought their dog in but only four of you can take it for a walk. Who should go?

TALKABOUT Assertiveness ... Making suggestions

Activity 15 'The negotiating game' worksheet

Name .... Date ....

 What does making suggestions mean?

 How could we make a suggestion? What do we need to remember?

TALKABOUT Assertiveness ... Making suggestions

Activity 16 The rules for making suggestions

Preparation

Photocopy the handout. Cut them to size if the group members are going to put them in their A5 fact book.

Instructions

- Explain to the group that you are going to consider the rules for making suggestions appropriately and effectively.

- Ask the group to consider why it is important to make suggestions to other people. Think about how it is best to do this assertively.

- What happens if we don't do this? How do we appear?

- Distribute the handout and discuss what it says.

Note on STAR plan: now complete a STAR plan for making suggestions. See Activity 10 for the instructions and worksheet.

TALKABOUT Assertiveness ... Making suggestions

Activity 16 'The rules for making suggestions' handout

Name .... Date ....

Making suggestions

How could we make suggestions?

 ✓ Wait for a pause in the conversation to give your idea and explain it

 ✓ Use a calm voice and speak clearly, remembering not to shout

 ✓ Try saying 'I think that ...' or 'Maybe we should ...' or 'Why don't we ...?'

 ✓ Remember to listen to other people's suggestions and respond appropriately

Why is this important?

It is important to be able to make suggestions clearly and appropriately to give our ideas and opinions effectively. We may have a suggestion that will help someone out or solve a problem.

If we don't tell people our ideas or suggestions then a decision or plan may not be reached. We might not be able to do what we really wanted to, which may make us feel sad or annoyed.

TALKABOUT Assertiveness ... Making suggestions

Activity 17 Suggestion time ... 'Suggestion indigestion' and more

Additional activities for making suggestions

- **Suggestion indigestion.** The group brainstorms lots of different situations where suggestions may need to be made. You may have some from Activity 15. Divide the group into pairs or small groups and give each one a situation to role play. Each pair or small group discusses how they should make suggestions in that scenario and then practises it before performing their role plays to the rest of the group.

- **Change one thing.** One group member is selected to go first and leave the room. The rest of the group members then all suggest something that could be changed in the room, eg someone takes off their shoes or a pot of pens is moved. The group decide which is the best suggestion, make the change and then call the group member back in. They must then try to guess what has changed. The game is repeated until everyone has had a turn to leave the room.

- **Compliment game.** One group member is asked to leave the room. The other group members then all suggest things that they like about that person or something they are good at. The group decide which is the best compliment and write it down. The group member is then called back in and someone reads them the compliment the group has decided on. They are asked what they thought about their compliment and how it made them feel. Repeat the game until all of the group members have had a chance to leave the room and receive a compliment.

- **Structures.** Explain to the group that the idea of this game is for them to collectively create an object using their bodies. Everyone needs to be involved and included in some way. Then the group must think of suggestions for what they could become and the best suggestion is chosen. The group member who made the suggestion then becomes the 'director' and gets the group to become the chosen structure by giving each person suggestions about their role or position. When the structure is complete, you could take a photograph so that the group can see how they have done. You could then try another group member's suggestion and they become the 'director'. Good structures to try are car, boat, train, aeroplane, bridge and toaster. Can the group then complete the movement of the structure too, eg an aeroplane taxiing down the runway?

TALKABOUT Assertiveness ... Refusing

Topic 5 Refusing

Activity 18 Saying 'no'

Preparation

You will need to photocopy the scenario cards, the 'no/yes' response cards and the headings for reasons why we need to say 'no'. Laminate them if you want to use them again.

You will also need to photocopy the worksheet – enlarge it to either A3 size for the group to complete or A4 for everyone to complete. You may also need scissors and glue.

Instructions

- Introduce the session by explaining to the group that you will be thinking about a new assertive skill – refusing.

- Take it in turns to read out one of the scenarios and consider whether the person should say 'yes' or 'no'.

- Consider how they should say 'no' and find an appropriate response from one of the 'no' speech bubble cards.

- The group then considers why it is appropriate to say 'no' in each situation. Is it because they don't agree with it? Or because they don't want to? Or is it because it is not right or safe?

- Sort the cards under the different headings.

- Complete the worksheet as a group with everyone's ideas or complete it individually.

TALKABOUT Assertiveness ... Refusing

Activity 18 'Saying "no"' scenario cards

George is a vegetarian. Ali offers him some of her ham sandwich.

Nick is working hard in his garden. He is enjoying himself. His friend Alex wants him to go to the pub but Nick doesn't want to go.

Matilda is baby-sitting for her aunt this evening. Her friend Amir asks her if she wants to go to the cinema.

Jan is not feeling well. She has recently been in hospital and is still not well enough to go outside. Bob asks her if she can help him out by walking his dog this evening. He has been asked to go in to work.

Darren is in a hurry – he has an appointment he has to get to. His friend Yuri asks him if he has time for a chat as he is feeling sad.

Amelia wants to miss work today and pretend that she is ill. She phones her friend Grace and suggests that they both go shopping instead of going to work.

TALKABOUT Assertiveness ... Refusing

Activity 18 'Saying "no"' scenario cards

Chuma suggests to his friend Lydia that they go swimming in the river. Lydia is not a strong swimmer.

Neil is hungry and wants a chocolate bar but doesn't have enough money to buy one. He asks his friend Matt to go to the shop and steal one for him.

Sue doesn't have anything pretty to wear to a party tonight so she asks her sister, Jo, if she can borrow one of her tops.

Lalla is bored and wants to play a trick on someone. She suggests that Sam hides in the cupboard and jumps out on their friend Becky. Sam knows that Becky is not feeling very happy today.

Lucy is walking into town. She notices an old lady struggling to cross a busy road. The old lady asks Lucy to help her.

John is playing with his friends. They suggest that it would be fun to go and play on the railway lines. John doesn't want to.

TALKABOUT Assertiveness ... Refusing

Activity 18 'Saying "no"' response cards

No

No thank you, I ...

No, I'm sorry ...

No, I don't want to because...

No, I think that is a bad idea ...

No, I can't do that because ...

Yes ...

OK!

TALKABOUT Assertiveness ... Refusing

Activity 18 'Saying "no"' response headings

Refusing ... why do we need to?

| It's not safe |

| I don't agree with it |

| I don't want to do it |

| I don't like it |

| It's not right |

| It would hurt someone else |

| I can't do it |

TALKABOUT Assertiveness ... Refusing

Activity 18 'Saying "no"' worksheet

Name .... Date ....

Refusing ... why do we need to?

There are 7 good reasons why we may want to refuse.
Can you remember them all?

1 ....
2 ....
3 ....
4 ....
5 ....
6 ....
7 ....

Refusing ... what could we say?

Activity 19 The rules for refusing

Preparation

Photocopy the handout. Cut them to size if the group members are going to put them in their A5 fact book.

You may want to prepare short role plays (modelling) of you and a co-facilitator having a conversation, or source a few video clips of people refusing in a conversation. You could use the refusing clips on the Talkabout DVD as an alternative to the modelling.

Instructions

- Explain to the group that you are going to consider the rules for refusing appropriately and effectively.

- The group facilitators can model inappropriate refusing, ie passively refusing and then aggressively refusing. Make sure that you model a scenario where a refusal is necessary, for example, one of the facilitators asks to borrow the other one's car as she has had another accident and written off yet another car!

- Ask the group to consider how the facilitator should refuse more assertively. What should they do?

- Then model the assertive way to refuse.

- Ask the group to consider why it is important to be able to refuse. What happens if we don't do this? How do we appear?

- Distribute the handout and discuss what it says.

Note on STAR plan: now complete a STAR plan for refusing. See Activity 10 for the instructions and worksheet.

TALKABOUT Assertiveness ... Refusing

Activity 19 'The rules for refusing' handout

Name ………………………………………………………….. Date ……………………….

Refusing

How should we refuse assertively?

 ✓ Stop and think – do you agree with what is being asked? Do you have a choice?

 ✓ Remember to use assertive body language to show that you are confident about what you say

 ✓ Use a calm voice and speak clearly

 ✓ Say 'no' and then, if appropriate, give a reason

Why is this important?

It is important to be able to refuse clearly and appropriately so that other people know what we think and feel. Sometimes we need to refuse because it is the safe or right thing to do. Sometimes we just can't do something and need to say 'no' and then apologise. If we don't refuse assertively, people may think we are weak or boring. They may also make us do something we don't want to.

TALKABOUT Assertiveness ... Refusing

Activity 20 The refusing game

Preparation

You will need the 'no' response cards from Activity 18.

Instructions

- Ask the group to remember all of the different ways you can say 'no'. You could have the 'no' response cards from Activity 18 in the middle of the table.

- Explain to the group that you are going to ask them, in turn, to do something and then, if they think it is right to refuse, they should say 'no' in an appropriate way.

- Start by asking every group member to do something very simple, eg 'Amy, can you stand up please?'

- Once everyone has had a turn at doing something reasonable, start asking the group members to do something unreasonable, for example:

    o   Go and put the waste-paper bin on your head.

    o   Can you say something mean to the person sitting next to you?

    o   Please will you go and find something in the room that doesn't belong to you and put it in your bag?

    o   Let's go and play near the motorway!

    o   Can you put your chair on that table and then stand on the chair?

    o   Can you try to take your friend's phone without her knowing and then phone someone?

- Ask the group how did it feel to say 'no'? What worked best?

Variation

Keep a diary over a week of the times you said 'no' or the times you said 'yes' but would have liked to refuse.

TALKABOUT Assertiveness ... Disagreeing

Topic 6 Disagreeing

Activity 21 The disagreeing game

Preparation

Photocopy and cut out the statement cards and the voting cards. You will need enough voting cards so that every group member has one of each. Laminate them if you want to use them again.

Photocopy the group record sheet.

Instructions

- Explain to the group that they are going to think about the new assertive topic of disagreeing, starting with a voting game.

- Give each group member a set of voting cards. Then read the first statement and ask the group members to vote by holding up the relevant card. Note down on the group record sheet how many of them agreed and disagreed.

- Continue reading a few of the statements and getting the group to vote. Then see if anyone has a statement they would like to ask the group to vote on.

- At the end of this task, look at the record sheet. Were there any statements which the whole group either agreed or disagreed on? What about ones where there was a divide? Discuss whether there is a compromise that could be made.

- Summarise by discussing disagreeing and saying that it is OK to disagree about something but other people's opinions may differ. We need to respect each other's views and give reasons why we agree or disagree. In the end, we may need to reach a compromise so that everyone is happy.

Variation

Instead of using the voting cards, you could designate one side of the room as 'agree' and another as 'disagree'. Then, when a statement is read out, the group members move to the side of the room corresponding to whether they agree or disagree.

TALKABOUT Assertiveness ... Disagreeing

Activity 21 'The disagreeing game' statement cards

Scary films are brilliant	Curry is the worst food
Football is boring	Homework is important
Rich people are happier than poorer people	Beetles are the best cars
Cats make the best pets	Christmas is the best time of year
Exercising is boring	Winter is better than summer

TALKABOUT Assertiveness ... Disagreeing

Activity 21 'The disagreeing game' voting cards

TALKABOUT Assertiveness ... Disagreeing

Activity 21 'The disagreeing game' group record sheet

The disagreeing game – group record

Statement	How many agree	How many disagree	I suggest... Is there a compromise?

TALKABOUT Assertiveness ... Disagreeing

Activity 22 Why is disagreeing important?

Preparation

Photocopy the worksheet and enlarge it to A3 size if you are completing this activity as a group. Photocopy at A4 size if the group members are completing them individually.

You may want to prepare short role plays (modelling) of you and a co-facilitator having a conversation, or source a few video clips of people disagreeing in a conversation. You could use the 'Disagreeing' clips on the Talkabout DVD as an alternative to the modelling.

Instructions

- Ask the group to watch you and your co-facilitator having a conversation. You should then model inappropriate disagreeing, ie passively disagreeing and then aggressively disagreeing. Make sure that you model a scenario where a disagreement is appropriate: for example, your co-facilitator thinks that living in the country is better than in the city where you live.

- Ask the group to consider how the facilitator should disagree more assertively. What should they do?

- Then model the assertive way to disagree.

- Next, ask the group to brainstorm different situations where they may want to disagree: for example, about what they have for dinner or something that is said in their news. Add the ideas to the worksheet.

- The group then considers why it is important to disagree: for example, so that other people know how we think and feel, or to get something that we would prefer. Write these reasons on the worksheet too.

- Finally, ask the group to think about what they could say. How might they start a sentence to disagree with someone or something? Get the group to think about this in pairs and maybe try out a few before feeding back their ideas to the group. Add them to the worksheet too.

TALKABOUT Assertiveness ... Disagreeing

Activity 22 'Why is disagreeing important?' worksheet

Name .... Date ....

Disagreeing ... why is it important?

? When should we disagree about something?

Disagreeing ... what could we say?

TALKABOUT Assertiveness ... Disagreeing

Activity 23 The rules for disagreeing

Preparation

Photocopy the handout. Cut them to size if the group members are going to put them in their A5 fact book.

You may also need the worksheet from Activity 22.

Instructions

- Explain to the group that you are going to consider the rules for disagreeing appropriately and effectively.

- Ask the group to think about the previous activity. Why might it be important to disagree and what could they say?

- Think about how they can disagree assertively and what they need to remember. What happens if we don't do this? How do we appear?

- Distribute the handout and discuss what it says.

Note on STAR plan: now complete a STAR plan for disagreeing. See Activity 10 for the instructions and worksheet.

TALKABOUT Assertiveness ... **Disagreeing**

Activity 23 'The rules for disagreeing' handout

Name .... Date ....

Disagreeing

How could we disagree?

 ✓ Stop and think, do you agree with what is being said or suggested?

 ✓ Remember to listen and respect other people's opinions. Is there a compromise?

 ✓ Use a calm voice and speak clearly. Remember to use assertive body language

 ✓ Try saying 'I'm sorry, I disagree ...' or 'Maybe we should ... instead'

Why is this important?

It is important to be able to disagree clearly and appropriately so that other people understand how we think and feel. We may have a better idea or a compromise that will make other people happy as well as us. If we don't disagree or tell people our opinions, we may not be able to do or get the things we would like. Other people might think we are weak or that we don't have any ideas.

TALKABOUT Assertiveness ... Disagreeing

Activity 24 Disagree dilemma

Preparation

Clear enough space in the room for the group to be able to move around and practise their role plays.

Instructions

- Consider some of the situations which you discussed in Activity 22 or think of some new ones.

- Divide the group into pairs and give each one a scenario. Each pair then thinks about how they could role play this scenario and how they can disagree assertively.

- Spend a few minutes with each pair, checking that they are showing the right skills before they perform their role play.

- When all of the pairs are ready, they take it in turns to show their role plays to the rest of the group and practise how to disagree appropriately.

- Repeat this activity as necessary until everyone feels confident. They may like to practise outside the group and feed back their successes and their difficulties in the next session.

TALKABOUT Assertiveness ... Complaining

Topic 7 Complaining

Activity 25 Complaining time

Preparation

Photocopy the worksheet. You may want to enlarge it to A3 size for the group to complete or have A4 copies for individuals to complete.

You may want to prepare short role plays (modelling), or source a few video clips, to demonstrate complaining in a conversation. You could use the 'Complaining' clip on the Talkabout DVD as an alternative to the modelling.

Instructions

- Introduce this skill by modelling inappropriate complaining. Make sure that you model a scenario where a complaint is necessary, eg your friend (co-facilitator) has sold you her old mobile phone (cell phone) but it doesn't charge, so you can't use it. She didn't tell you this before you bought it from her.

- In the first scenario, the facilitator should not complain and just accept the situation, maybe even blaming herself for not checking the phone first. Ask the group what they think went wrong. What should have happened?

- Then model the same scenario but complain passively and then aggressively. Ask the group to consider after each one how the facilitator should complain more assertively. What should they do?

- In the final scenario, model the assertive way to complain. Ask the group what did the facilitator do differently? Can the group summarise what assertive complaining looks like?

- Next, discuss when it is important to complain: for example, when something is faulty or wrong, or when you have been misled by something or someone.

- Why is it important to complain? Consider such things as our consumer rights and our human rights.

- Finally, complete the worksheet either as a group with everyone's ideas or individually.

TALKABOUT Assertiveness ... Complaining

Activity 25 'Complaining time' worksheet

Name .... Date ....

When should we complain? Can you list a few ideas?

1 ....
2 ....
3 ....
4 ....

How should we complain? What do we need to remember?

TALKABOUT Assertiveness ... Complaining

Activity 26 The rules for complaining

Preparation

Photocopy the handout. Cut them to size if the group members are going to put them in their A5 fact book.

Instructions

- Explain to the group that you are going to consider the rules for complaining appropriately and effectively.

- Think about the previous activity and what we learned about how we should complain. Consider things like choosing the right person to talk to, using our assertive body language and voice, stating the reason why we are complaining, but listening to the other person and respecting what they have to say too.

- What happens if we don't do this? How do we appear?

- Distribute the handout and discuss what it says.

Note on STAR plan: now complete a STAR plan for complaining. See Activity 10 for the instructions and worksheet.

Activity 26 'The rules for complaining' handout

Name .... Date ....

Complaining

How should we complain assertively?

✓ Stop and think – who should you talk to? What are your rights?

✓ Remember to use assertive body language to show that you are confident in what you say

✓ Use a calm voice and speak clearly

✓ Explain why you are not happy. Try saying 'I am not happy because …'

Why is this important?

It is sometimes important to complain if we feel something is not right or we have been misled or sold something faulty. It is important to do this clearly and appropriately so that other people know what we think and feel.

If we don't complain assertively, people may take advantage of us and think we are weak.

Activity 27 The complaining game

Preparation

You will need a large sheet of paper and some pens.

Instructions

- Ask the group to remember all of the different times it is important to be able to complain. Write down a list of scenarios to role play.

- Divide the group into pairs and give each one a scenario. Each pair then thinks about how they could role play this scenario and how they can complain assertively.

- Spend a few minutes with each pair before they perform their role play to the others.

- When all of the pairs are ready, they take it in turns to show their role play to the rest of the group.

- Repeat this activity as necessary until everyone feels confident. They may like to practise outside the group and feed back their successes and their difficulties in the next session.

Variation

The group members could keep a diary over a week of the times they needed to complain or would have liked to complain but didn't. What have they learned from this?

TALKABOUT Assertiveness ... Apologising

Topic 8 Apologising

Activity 28 Saying sorry

Preparation

Photocopy the worksheet. You may want to enlarge it to A3 size for the group to complete.

You may want to prepare short role plays (modelling), or source a few video clips, to demonstrate apologising in a conversation. You could use the 'Apologising' clip on the Talkabout DVD as an alternative to the modelling.

Instructions

- Introduce this skill by modelling inappropriate apologising. Make sure that you model a scenario where an apology is necessary, eg your friend (your co-facilitator) kicks you while talking to you.

- In the first scenario, the facilitator does not apologise at all, even though the other facilitator says 'Ow!' Ask the group what they think went wrong. What should have happened? The group will say that she should have said 'sorry'.

- Then model the same scenario but, this time, the facilitator apologises inappropriately. The following order works well.

    o They apologise but say it insincerely and carry on (they didn't sound like they meant it).

    o They apologise nicely but then blame the other person, eg 'If you move your leg, it won't happen again' (they don't take responsibility).

    o They apologise nicely but then repeat the action several times (they don't learn from their actions).

    o They apologise too much and embarrass the other person.

- Ask the group to consider after each scenario how well the facilitator did with the apology. What should they have done differently?

- In the final scenario, model the assertive way to apologise. What did the facilitator do differently? Can the group summarise what assertive apologising looks like?

- Finally, complete the worksheet either as a group with everyone's ideas or individually.

TALKABOUT Assertiveness ... Apologising

Activity 28 'Saying sorry' worksheet

Name .... Date ....

What does a good apology mean? Can you list a few ideas?

1 ....
2 ....
3 ....
4 ....
5 ....

 **Why do we need to apologise?**

TALKABOUT Assertiveness ... Apologising

Activity 29 The sorry scale

Preparation

Photocopy and cut out the cards. There are two blank ones for you to fill in if you wish. You may want to laminate them if you want to use them again.

Photocopy the worksheet. You may want to enlarge it to A3 size to collate the ideas as a group.

Instructions

- Explain to the group that you are going to think about the different ways we say 'sorry'. You can introduce the concept of the 'big sorry' and the 'little sorry'. If you want to add a middle one, this is also OK.

- The group members take it in turns to choose a card and read the scenario. How would you apologise? Is it short and sweet (a little sorry)? Or does it need much more effort with some evidence of regret and actions to remedy the situation (a big sorry)?

- Talk about times when the group members have had to say 'sorry' recently. What did they do? Was it a big sorry or a little sorry? What did they say? Do they think they should have done something differently?

- Then write down the ideas on the group worksheet or they can complete the worksheet individually.

TALKABOUT Assertiveness ... Apologising

Activity 29 'The sorry scale' cards

BIG sorry	Little sorry
You have just bumped into your friend while walking down the corridor.	You have borrowed your friend's phone and dropped it by mistake and the screen is now cracked.
Your mum asked you to walk the dog while she was at work but you forgot.	You have just driven your car into your neighbour's car while reversing. There is a big dent in his car now.
Your neighbour has just been round to complain about your music last night. You had friends visiting and didn't realise the music was so loud.	You have just knocked your friend's cup of tea all over her laptop.

Activity 29 'The sorry scale' cards (continued)

You have forgotten it is your friend's birthday.	Your friend has come round for dinner. You have cooked beef lasagne but forgot that she is a vegetarian.
Your boss asked you to buy milk on the way to work today. You forgot.	You teased your friend this morning about her new hair cut. You meant it as a joke but now realise that she is upset.
You call out 'Hello' to your friend as you walk into the room but don't realise he is on the phone.	You accidently step on your friend's shoe.

TALKABOUT Assertiveness ... Apologising

Activity 29 'The sorry scale' worksheet

Name .... Date ....

Saying sorry

I'm sorry!

❶ 'Little sorry' ...

This means we may have done something little by accident.
We have not hurt anyone's feelings and there is no lasting damage.

A little sorry means we should ...

....

....

....

I'm sorry!

❷ 'Big sorry' ...

This means we may have done something much more serious.
We may have hurt someone's feelings or damaged something.

A BIG sorry means we should ...

....

....

....

TALKABOUT Assertiveness ... Apologising

Activity 30 The rules for apologising

Preparation

Photocopy the handout. Cut them to size if the group members are going to put them in their A5 fact book.

Instructions

- Explain to the group that you are going to consider the rules for apologising appropriately and effectively.

- Think about the previous activity and what we learned about how we should apologise. Consider things like how big the sorry should be and whether we need to do something to make up for it. Also think about our assertive body language and voice.

- Discuss 'the three Rs' – regret, responsibility and remedy.

- What happens if we don't do this? How do we appear?

- Distribute the handout and discuss what it says.

Note on STAR plan: now complete a STAR plan for apologising. See Activity 10 for the instructions and worksheet.

Activity 30 'The rules for apologising' handout

Name .... Date ....

Apologising

How should we apologise assertively?

 ✓ Stop and think – who should you apologise to? Does it need to be a big or a little sorry?

 ✓ Remember to use assertive body language to show that you mean what you are saying

 ✓ Use a sincere tone of voice and express regret

 ✓ Take responsibility. Try saying 'I am sorry – that was my fault' and, if appropriate, do something to make up for it

Why is this important?

It is important to apologise if we have made a mistake or upset someone. We should do it quickly and with meaning so that people know we are really sorry.

If we don't apologise assertively, people will think we are selfish and will not want to be friends with us.

TALKABOUT Assertiveness ... Apologising

Activity 31 The apologising game

Preparation

None needed.

Instructions

- Ask the group to remember all of the different times it is important to be able to say 'sorry'. Consider the examples that were discussed in Activity 29.

- Divide the group into pairs and give each one a scenario. Each pair then thinks about how they could role play this scenario and how they can apologise appropriately and assertively.

- Spend a few minutes with each pair before they perform their role play to the others.

- When all of the pairs are ready, they take it in turns to show their role play to the rest of the group.

- Repeat this activity as necessary until everyone feels confident. They may like to practise outside the group and feed back their successes and their difficulties in the next session.

Variation

The group members could keep a diary for a week of the times they needed to apologise or would have liked to apologise but didn't. What have they learned from this?

TALKABOUT Assertiveness ... Requesting explanations

Topic 9 Requesting explanations

Activity 32 Requesting time

Preparation

Photocopy the worksheet. You may want to enlarge it to A3 size to complete as a group.

You may want to prepare short role plays (modelling) of you and your co-facilitator having a conversation (see below), or source a few video clips of people requesting an explanation. You could use the 'Requesting an explanation' clip on the Talkabout DVD as an alternative to the modelling.

Instructions

- Introduce this skill by modelling inappropriate requesting of explanations. Make sure that you model a scenario where this skill is necessary. For example, your friend (co-facilitator) has said that everyone is meeting tomorrow for lunch at a new café in town but you're not sure where that is, what time to meet or who is going.

- In the first scenario, one facilitator should try to request the information but does it passively. For example, they may say 'Oh, I think I know where you mean' and 'Well, I have from 12 until one for lunch, so that should be OK', etc. Ask the group what they think went wrong. What should have happened?

- Then model the same scenario but, this time, the facilitator requests aggressively. For example, they may say 'Well that's a stupid idea, I don't know where that place is', 'Are you going to tell me where it is or not?' and 'Well, I only have an hour for lunch, so it better be in that time'. Ask the group if that was better. The facilitator was more direct but how did the co-facilitator feel? What should have happened to get the information needed more assertively?

- In the final scenario, model the assertive way to request explanations. What did the facilitators do differently? Can the group members summarise what assertive requesting looks like?

- Discuss when it is important to request explanations: for example, when we are unsure what something means or what is expected of us.

- Why is it important to request explanations? For example, to have all the information, to be able to make choices, and to know what is happening.

- Finally, complete the worksheet either as a group with everyone's ideas or individually.

312

TALKABOUT Assertiveness ... Requesting explanations

Activity 32 'Requesting time' worksheet

Name .... Date ....

Requesting explanations

When might we request explanations? Can you list a few ideas?

1 ....
2 ....
3 ....
4 ....
5 ....

 How should we request information? What do we need to remember?

TALKABOUT Assertiveness ... Requesting explanations

Activity 33 The rules for requesting explanations

Preparation

Photocopy the handout. Cut them to size if the group members are going to put them in their A5 fact book.

Instructions

- Explain to the group that they are going to consider the rules for requesting explanations appropriately and effectively.

- Think about the previous activity and what they learned about how we should request an explanation. Consider things like apologising because you haven't understood, asking a clear question, using assertive body language and voice, saying 'thank you' if someone responds with a good explanation.

- What happens if we don't do this? How do we appear?

- Distribute the handout and discuss what it says.

Note on STAR plan: now complete a STAR plan for requesting explanations. See Activity 10 for the instructions and worksheet.

TALKABOUT Assertiveness ... Requesting explanations

Activity 33 'The rules for requesting explanations' handout

Name .... Date ....

Requesting explanations

How should we request explanations assertively?

 ✓ Stop and think – do you understand what has been said or asked of you?

 ✓ Use a calm voice, speak clearly and remember to use assertive body language

 ✓ Ask a question or for an explanation. Try saying 'I'm sorry I don't understand, please could you explain?'

 ✓ Remember to say 'thank you'

! Why is this important?

It is important to request explanations if we don't understand something or if we need more information. It is important to do this clearly and appropriately so that other people can understand us and give us the right explanation. If we don't request explanations assertively, people may not know that we need more information or they may think that we are rude. We may feel confused or not be able to complete tasks.

TALKABOUT Assertiveness ... Requesting explanations

Activity 34 The requesting game

Preparation

You will need a large sheet of paper and some pens.

Instructions

- Ask the group to remember all of the different times it is important to request explanations. Write down a list of scenarios to role play.

- Divide the group into pairs and give each one a scenario. Each pair then thinks about how they could role play this scenario and how they can request assertively.

- Spend a few minutes with each pair before they perform their role play to the others.

- When all of the pairs are ready, they take it in turns to show their role play to the rest of the group.

- Repeat this activity as necessary until everyone feels confident. They may like to practise outside the group and feed back their successes and their difficulties in the next session.

Variation

The group members could keep a diary for a week of the times they were able to or would have liked to request explanations but didn't. What have they learned from this?

TALKABOUT Assertiveness ... What am I like

Topic 10 My assertiveness

Activity 35 Assertiveness ... what am I like? (part 2)

Preparation

Photocopy new assessment sheets. Make sure that you have the completed assessment sheets and target sheets from Activity 6, one for each group member.

Instructions

- Ask the group to consider how they have got on over the last few weeks and whether they think they have improved.

- As a group, go through the 'What am I like?' assessment sheet and ask where they would rate themselves now.

- Then ask the group members to think individually about where they are with their assertiveness skills now and to mark this on their sheet. They may want to sit in different parts of the room to be more private.

- Then discuss with each group member how they have rated themselves and compare this with their original assessment sheet.

- The group members are then given a certificate of achievement.

TALKABOUT Assertiveness... How did I do?

Activity 35 'Assertiveness' assessment worksheet

Name .... Date ....

Assertiveness ... what am I like at it?

	Never good	Not very good	Quite good	Very good
① Expressing feelings *(I feel..)*				
② Standing up for yourself *(This is ME!)*				
③ Making suggestions *(I suggest..)*				
④ Refusing *(NO!)*				
⑤ Disagreeing *(I disagree..)*				
⑥ Complaining *(This soup is cold)*				
⑦ Apologising *(I'm sorry!)*				
⑧ Requesting explanations *(I'd like to ask)*				

TALKABOUT Assertiveness ... What am I like?

Certificate of Achievement

THIS IS TO CERTIFY THAT

....

HAS COMPLETED TALKABOUT LEVEL 4

ASSERTIVENESS SKILLS

SIGNED .... DATE ....

Group cohesion games

It is recommended that a group cohesion game is played to start and end every session. This helps to focus the group members and it ensures that everyone leaves feeling relaxed at the end of the session. A good group cohesion game is fun, simple and stress-free. It should be a game that everyone can take part in and no one is left out. It can be linked to the topic you are currently working on or it could be something completely unrelated.

Some of our favourites are:

- The zoo game
- I went to market
- Horrible sandwiches
- Change one thing
- Steal the keys
- Add an action
- Pass the mime
- Pass the bomb
- Structures
- The praise game

For instructions on how to play any of the above games, see *Talkabout for Adults* (Kelly, 2014), *Talkabout for Teenagers* (Kelly & Bains, 2009) or the *Talkabout group cohesion cards* (Kelly, 2011d).

Some new ideas for games are given overleaf.

TALKABOUT

 ### The human knot

For this game, you will need at least four people but no more than six. Stand the group in a circle, all facing inwards. Ask everyone to put one arm out into the circle and hold the hand of someone else in the group. Next ask the group to all put their other arm in and hold hands with someone different. When everyone has hold of two hands, explain that now you want the group to untangle themselves so that everyone is standing back in a circle with straight arms. The group can twist and step over each other in order to untangle but must never let go of each other's hands. If you have a large group, it can be fun to divide into two groups and have a race. This may take a while … but is always achievable!

 ### Pass the hoop

For this game, you will need a hula hoop. Stand the group members in a circle, all facing inwards, and ask them to hold hands. The hoop is placed over the group facilitator's arm before they hold hands. The idea of the game is to pass the hoop around the circle and back to the start without letting go of anyone's hands. The group members will need to help each other to get everyone through the hoop. Once you have got all the way round, see if you can go back the other way.

 ### The dice decider

For this game, you will need an even number in the group, so a facilitator may decide not to play. You will also need a dice. The group should sit in a circle on chairs. Each group member is then given a number. You will need two group members to be the same number, eg in a group of six, you will have two group members who are a 1, two who are a 2 and two who are a 3.

Group members then take it in turns to roll the dice. If a 1 is thrown then the group members who are a 1 both stand up and run around the circle back to their chair. The person who is back to their seat first wins. The game continues until everyone has had a few turns.

 ### Call-and-response games

Some call-and-response games are detailed in Level 2 The Way We Talk in this book but they also make good cohesion games. The group members sit or stand in a circle and begin by creating a beat by clapping hands, tapping thighs or stamping feet. The group facilitator then calls out, for example, 'Good morning Sarah', keeping to the beat. The group then repeats this back. The group facilitator continues for a while, then hands over to anyone else who would like a turn.

Record forms

Contents	page
Plan of intervention	324
Session plan and evaluation	325
Individual target sheet	326
How did I do? record sheet	327

TALKABOUT ... Record forms

Plan of intervention

Group _____ Date _____

Topic _____

Week	Plan	Equipment	Your notes

TALKABOUT ... Record forms

Session plan and evaluation

Group _____ Date _____

Topic _____ Session number _____

Members present _____

Activity	Plan	Evaluation
Starter activity		
How am I feeling? activity		
Main activities		
Finishing activity		

Completed by _____ Date _____

TALKABOUT ... Record forms

Individual target sheet

My name _____ Date _____

My aim is to _____

What I will be doing _____

My targets	1 Skill not present	2 Skill emerging with prompting	3 Skill emerging with occasional prompting	4 Skill present in a structured situation	5 Skill present in some other situations	6 Skill present and consistent across most situations

How did I do? _____

Signed _____ Date _____

TALKABOUT ... Record forms

'How did I do?' record sheet

Name _____

😊 I did well   😐 I did OK   ☹ It was hard

Code:
✓✓ = skill achieved
✓ = skill emerging
✗ = skill not present

Date	How did I do? 😊 😐 ☹			Evaluation of main activity	Comments	Signed

TALKABOUT References

References

Gray C (1994) *The New Social Story Book*, Future Horizons, Arlington, Texas.

Kelly A (1996) *TALKABOUT: A Social Communication Skills Package*, 1st edn, Speechmark Publishing, Milton Keynes.

Kelly A (2000) *Working with Adults with a Learning Disability*, Speechmark Publishing, Milton Keynes.

Kelly A (2003) *TALKABOUT Activities*, Speechmark Publishing, Milton Keynes.

Kelly A (2004) *TALKABOUT Relationships*, Speechmark Publishing, Milton Keynes.

Kelly A (2006) *TALKABOUT DVD*, Speechmark Publishing, Milton Keynes.

Kelly A (2011a) *TALKABOUT for Children 1: Developing Self-awareness and Self-esteem*, Speechmark Publishing, Milton Keynes.

Kelly A (2011b) *TALKABOUT for Children 2: Developing Social Skills*, Speechmark Publishing, Milton Keynes.

Kelly A (2011c) *TALKABOUT Posters*, Speechmark Publishing, Milton Keynes.

Kelly A (2011d) *Talkabout Cards: Group Cohesion Activities*, Speechmark Publishing, Milton Keynes.

Kelly A (2013) *TALKABOUT for Children 3: Friendship Skills*, Speechmark Publishing, Milton Keynes.

Kelly A & Green A (2014) *TALKABOUT for Adults: Developing Self-awareness and Self-esteem*, Speechmark Publishing, Milton Keynes.

Kelly A & Sains B (2009) *TALKABOUT for Teenagers*, Speechmark Publishing, Milton Keynes.

Kelly A & Sains B (2010) *TALKABOUT Assessment*, Speechmark Publishing, Milton Keynes.

Kelly A & Sains B (2011) *TALKABOUT Board Game*, Speechmark Publishing, Milton Keynes.

TALKABOUT Index

Index

Index	Section	Activity number	Page
aggressive behaviour	Assertiveness	2, 4	240, 249
answering questions	Conversations	13–15	203
the rules	Conversations	13	203
apologising	Assertiveness	28–31	301
game	Assertiveness	31	309
the rules	Assertiveness	30	308
are you open or closed?	Conversations	14	207
'asking Alex' game	Conversations	15	206
asking questions	Conversations	12, 14, 15	195, 12, 205
the rules	Conversations	12	195
assertiveness	Assertiveness	1–35	236
assessment	Assertiveness	6, 35	255, 315
plan	Assertiveness	6	257
scale	Assertiveness	1	236
what am I like? (part 1)	Assertiveness	6	255
what am I like? (part 2)	Assertiveness	35	315
what does assertiveness look like?	Assertiveness	2	241
what is assertiveness?	Assertiveness	1	236
assessment	Assessment	–	19
being aggressive	Assertiveness	4	249
being assertive	Assertiveness	5	251
being passive	Assertiveness	3	247
being relevant	Conversations	16–18	207
blindfold game	Body Language	8	56
body language	Body Language	1–46	36
assessment	Body Language	6, 46	48, 128
plan	Body Language	6	52
what am I like? (part 1)	Body Language	6	50
what am I like? (part 2)	Body Language	46	130
what is it?	Body Language	3	37
build a story activity	Conversations	18	216
call-and-response games	Group cohesion	–	320

TALKABOUT Index

Index	Section	Activity number	Page
certificate of achievement	All	–	130, 162, 230, 314
change one thing	Assertiveness	17	277
change places if …	Conversations	6	184
change the topic activity	Conversations	18	214
clarity	The Way We Talk	7	151
closer to you?	Body Language	25	88
comic strips (strategy 2)	Introduction	–	12
complaining	Assertiveness	25–27	296
game	Assertiveness	27	300
the rules	Assertiveness	26	300
time	Assertiveness	25	296
compliment game	Assertiveness	17	277
conversation critic	Conversations	23	226
conversational skills	Conversations	1–25	168
assessment	Conversations	3	176
plan	Conversations	3	176
what am I like? (part 1)	Conversations	3	176
what am I like? (part 2)	Conversations	25	229
what are they?	Conversations	1	168
why worry about them?	Conversations	2	172
dice decider game	Group cohesion	–	320
different feelings	Body Language	15	69
different gestures	Body Language	20	79
different postures	Body Language	39	116
disagree dilemma	Assertiveness	24	295
disagreeing	Assertiveness	21–24	287
game	Assertiveness	21	287
the rules	Assertiveness	23	283
distance	Body Language	23–27	85
the rules	Body Language	26	90
dotty about … dinosaurs	Conversations	17	212
dressed to impress	Body Language	45	126
emotions recap	Assertiveness	7	258

TALKABOUT Index

Index	Section	Activity number	Page
ending conversations	Conversations	21–24	220
the rules	Conversations	22	223
'ending Eddie' game	Conversations	24	228
ending time	Conversations	24	228
environment (strategy 1)	Introduction	–	14
evaluation form	Record forms	–	321
express yourself	Assertiveness	11	266
expressing feelings	Assertiveness	7–11	258
the rules	Assertiveness	9	262
eye contact	Body Language	7–12	57
the rules	Body Language	10	61
face your emotions	Body Language	17	76
facial expression	Body Language	13–17	67
the rules	Body Language	16	68
feelings	Assertiveness	7–11	260
fidgeting	Body Language	33–35	107
the rules	Body Language	35	111
fluency	The Way We Talk	9	157
format of session	Introduction	–	19
four step plan	Introduction	–	13
fruit salad game	Conversations	6	184
gesture	Body Language	18–22	74
the rules	Body Language	21	77
give us a hand	Body Language	22	83
good speaking, the rules	The Way We Talk	10	157
group cohesion games	Group cohesion	–	319
group work (strategy 8)	Introduction	–	13
hierarchy of social skills	Introduction	–	9
'how did I do?' record sheet	Record forms	–	325
how do we sound?	The Way We Talk	3	139
human knot game	Group cohesion	–	320
'I went to the market' game	Conversations	6, 11	184, 194
'I went to the Moon' game	Conversations	11	194

TALKABOUT Index

Index	Section	Activity number	Page
in the manner of the word	Body Language	4	43
intonation	The Way We Talk	8	153
learning to do good speaking	The Way We Talk	11	159
learning to look	Body Language	11	62
linking words activity	Conversations	18	214
listen to me!	The Way We Talk	1	132
listen to my starters	Conversations	7	185
listen to the ending	Conversations	21	219
listening	Conversations	4–6	179
listening time	Conversations	6	184
the rules	Conversations	4	179
look and listen	Conversations	5	182
looking good!	Body Language	43	122
making suggestions	Assertiveness	15–17	272
the rules	Assertiveness	16	275
media (strategy 6)	Introduction	–	13
mind the gap!	Body Language	27	92
modelling (strategy 7)	Introduction	–	13
musical starters game	Conversations	9	190
my clarity	The Way We Talk	7	151
my fluency	The Way We Talk	9	155
my intonation	The Way We Talk	8	153
my rate	The Way We Talk	6	148
my STAR plan for expressing feelings	Assertiveness	10	264
my volume	The Way We Talk	5	145
negotiating game	Assertiveness	15	272
paralinguistic skills	The Way We Talk	1–12	132–61
pass the greeting game	Conversations	9	190
pass the hoop game	Group cohesion	–	340
pass the mic game	Conversations	11	194
passive behaviour	Assertiveness	2, 3	241, 247
personal appearance	Body Language	42–45	120–26
the rules	Body Language	44	124
plan of intervention form	Record forms	–	322

TALKABOUT Index

Index	Section	Activity number	Page
planning intervention sheet	Assessment	–	31
poor communication	Body Language	7	53
posture	Body Language	36–41	111
thermometer	Body Language	38	116
the rules	Body Language	40	119
question time	Conversations	15	206
questions	Conversations	12–15	195–206
rate of speech	The Way We Talk	6	150
record form	Forms	–	321
refusing	Assertiveness	18–20	278
game	Assertiveness	20	286
the rules	Assertiveness	19	284
relevance	Conversations	16–18	207
the rules	Conversations	16	207
time	Conversations	18	214
'relevant Robyn' game	Conversations	18	214
repairing	Conversations	19, 20	215, 219
the rules	Conversations	19	215
time	Conversations	20	219
requesting explanations	Assertiveness	32–34	310
game	Assertiveness	34	314
time	Assertiveness	32	310
the rules	Assertiveness	33	312
reward system (strategy 5)	Introduction	–	16
role play (strategy 7)	Introduction	–	15
running a group	Introduction	–	16
saying 'no'	Assertiveness	18	278
saying sorry	Assertiveness	28	281
self-assessment	Assessment	–	32
self-awareness and self-esteem interview	Assessment	–	21
session plan form	Forms	–	323
setting up a group	Introduction	–	15
'Simon says' game	Conversations	6	184

TALKABOUT Index

Index	Section	Activity number	Page
social skills assessment	Assessment	–	24
social stories (strategy 3)	Introduction	–	16
sorry scale	Assertiveness	29	203
stand by Houston!	Assertiveness	14	271
standing tall	Assertiveness	12	267
standing up for yourself	Assertiveness	12–14	267
the rules	Assertiveness	13	269
STAR plan	Assertiveness	10	264
starting a conversation	Conversations	7–9	185–90
starting time	Conversations	9	190
the rules	Conversations	8	187
'starting up Sam' game	Conversations	9	190
stop and look	Body Language	12	66
strategies for intervention	Introduction	–	16
structures game	Assertiveness	17	277
suggestion indigestion	Assertiveness	17	277
suggestion time	Assertiveness	17	277
taking time	Conversations	11	194
taking turns	Conversations	10, 11	191, 194
'taking turns Toni' game	Conversations	11	194
Talkabout resource list	Introduction	–	8
target sheet	Record forms	–	324
tell a story game	Conversations	6	184
tell me a story game	Conversations	24	228
that's a close one!	Body Language	24	87
the way we talk	The Way We Talk	1–12	134
assessment	The Way We Talk	4, 12	142, 161
plan	The Way We Talk	4	148
what am I like? (part 1)	The Way We Talk	4	144
what am I like? (part 2)	The Way We Talk	12	163
theory of Talkabout	Introduction	–	10
time to pose!	Body Language	41	121
to touch or not to touch?	Body Language	32	105

TALKABOUT Index

Index	Section	Activity number	Page
touch	Body Language	28–32	95
control	Body Language	29	97
the rules	Body Language	31	103
turn taking	Conversations	10, 11	193, 196
the rules	Conversations	10	193
twenty questions game	Conversations	15	208
visual cue (strategy 4)	Introduction	–	16
volume	The Way We Talk	5	147
walk this way	Body Language	37	115
watch me fidget!	Body Language	33	117
watch my appearance!	Body Language	42	122
watch my eyes!	Body Language	7	53
watch my face!	Body Language	13	67
watch my hands!	Body Language	18	77
watch my posture!	Body Language	36	113
watch my touch!	Body Language	28	95
watch that man	Body Language	2	38
watch the distance!	Body Language	23	87
watch us talk!	Body Language	1	36
what could I do?	Assertiveness	8	259
what happens to our bodies when …?	Body Language	5	46
why do people fidget?	Body Language	34	109
why is disagreeing important?	Assertiveness	22	293
why is eye contact important?	Body Language	9	57
why is facial expression important?	Body Language	14	69
why is gesture important?	Body Language	19	79
why is good speaking important?	The Way We Talk	2	137
why is touch important?	Body Language	30	101
yes/no game	Conversations	15	208
zoo game	Conversations	6	186